W0246715

TOP **10**
VIENNA

CONTENTS

Top 10 of Everything

Area by Area

Streetsmart

VIENNA

INTRODUCING

Stephansdom

WELCOME TO
VIENNA

Grand, captivating, irresistible: that's Vienna. Here you can tour regal palaces, peruse art in world-class museums and linger over cake in a 19th-century coffee house – all in one day. Don't want to miss a thing? With Top 10 Vienna, you'll enjoy the very best the city has to offer.

The former capital of the Habsburg Empire and the modern-day capital of Austria, Vienna is one of Europe's most absorbing cities. Over seven centuries of Habsburg rule has bequeathed this city on the Danube with an imperial grandeur that's second to none in Central Europe.

This clan of emperors and kings left behind mammoth complexes such as the museum-stuffed Hofburg, Baroque Schönbrunn and many of the cultural institutions and classic churches with which Vienna overflows. The magnificent Belvedere plays second fiddle to

Enjoying coffee and cake in Vienna

such splendour but would be a star attraction in any other city, while the grand façades of the Ringstrasse lend old Wien (Vienna in German) a 19th-century splendour that befits an imperial capital. Vienna, in short, dazzles with the confidence of an erstwhile epicentre of power.

But Vienna isn't all about grand architecture and treasure-filled palaces. There's something more subtle in the air here: the rousing tones of Mozart, Mahler and Strauss drifting across Vienna's squares; the citrusy smell of wines wafting down from the vineyards that fringe the city; the sweet aroma of coffee and cake tempting passersby. Culture is

also the oxygen of the capital, from projects like the multi-coloured Hundertwasserhaus to the work of world-renowned painters hanging in some of Europe's most respected galleries. The swish of a ball dress, the rigid trot of one of the city's famous Lipizzaner horses, the sizzle of schnitzel on the skillet – the mosaic of Viennese life is rich and fascinating.

So, where to start? With Top 10 Vienna, of course. This pocket-sized guide gets to the heart of the city with simple lists of 10, expert local knowledge and comprehensive maps, helping you turn an ordinary trip into an extraordinary one.

THE STORY OF
VIENNA

From modest beginnings as a Roman garrison to the epicentre of the Habsburg Empire and now one of the world's most liveable and green cities, Vienna has come a long way in the last 2,000 years. Here's the story of how it came to be.

The 14th-century Habsburg ruler Rudolf IV, Duke of Austria

A City is Born

Vienna started life in the 1st century CE as Roman Vindabona, a military town situated at a natural crossing point on the River Danube. This later grew into a settlement of 30,000 people – today, much of Vienna's inner city centre is located on Vindabona's old stone streets. The only remnants of Roman Vienna can be found on Michaelerplatz, where a part of excavation works has been left uncovered.

The Habsburg Centuries

Vienna had a short spell as the capital of the Babenberg Dynasty, but it wasn't until 1273, when

Rudolf von Habsburg was elected Holy Roman Emperor and made his capital Vienna, that the city started to enjoy real power. The Habsburgs dominated Vienna and much of Central and Southeastern Europe for over seven centuries. From their capital, they married and battled their way to an empire stretching from the Balkans to the Baltic.

By the 15th century, Vienna was one of the most important cities in Europe. Under the Habsburgs, a multitude of palaces, churches and seats of learning were built, and many ongoing Viennese traditions, such as coffee houses, the Spanish Riding School and grand balls, were established. The city also saw huge influences from other parts of Europe as Czechs, Croats, Slovenes and Hungarians flocked to the capital.

Siege of Vienna by the Turks in 1683 by Romeyn de Hooghe

Foreign Threats

The greatest threat to Vienna's prosperity came from the Ottoman Turks, who overran the Balkans in the 16th and 17th centuries. They dubbed the Habsburg capital the "City of the Golden Apple", a precious fruit they were determined to taste. The first siege of Vienna came in 1529 and lasted 18 days – but it did not break the city's resolve. The Ottomans tried to take Vienna again in 1683, but once again they failed. As the Turkish threat abated, Vienna entered its Golden Age, a centre of both power and the arts.

Napoleon and Metternich

Vienna was occupied by Napoleon Bonaparte twice, in 1805 and 1809, but it also bore witness to the Congress of Vienna in 1815, after Napoleon's defeat at Waterloo, which redrew the map of Europe. One of the biggest players at the congress was Chancellor Metternich, a wily, rather eccentric character whose repression of groups across the Austrian Empire dominated the first half of the 19th century – ultimately leading to the ecomonic-induced revolutions that took place across Central Europe in 1848.

Moments in History

15–20 CE
The Romans establish a garrison town on a ford on the River Danube, naming it Vindabona.

1273
The Habsburgs take control of Vienna, dominating the city and the entire region for the next 700 years.

1683
The second Ottoman siege of Vienna fails to break the Habsburg capital. Turkish general Mustafa is put to the sword by the sultan for his failure.

1805 & 1809
Napoleon twice occupies Vienna, in 1805, after the Battle of Austerlitz, and in 1809, following the Battle of Wagram.

1857
Vienna's city walls are pulled down, marking the beginning of the city's expansion and modernization, including construction of the Ringstrasse.

1918
The Habsburg Empire ends as states such as Czechoslovakia and Yugoslavia are created following World War I.

1920s
Vienna experiences significant unrest, as communists attempt to take over the city in what is commonly known as the "Red Vienna" period.

1938
Adolf Hitler annexes Austria for the Third Reich, an event that is welcomed by the majority of the population of Vienna.

1955
Austria declares itself a neutral state, but despite this it joins the EU four decades later.

2022
Vienna's population surpasses two million people for the first time, reflecting the city's dynamic economic growth in the early 21st century.

Johann Strauss (1825–99) at a court ball in Vienna

A Cultural Powerhouse
The 18th and 19th centuries saw Vienna become the classical music capital of Europe, when a raft of illustrious composers contributed to the cultural blossoming that was taking place here. Wolfgang Amadeus Mozart, Joseph Haydn, Ludwig van Beethoven, Franz Schubert, Johann and Josef Strauss, Johannes Brahms and Gustav Mahler all lived and worked in the imperial capital at some point.

It was during this period that Vienna's most famous Baroque palaces and churches, such as the Belvedere and Schloss Schönbrunn, were built, while in the 19th century, the city also served as the creative hub for some of the world's best-known artists and writers, including Gustav Klimt, Egon Schiele, Franz Kafka, Adolf Loos and Hand Hoffman. The turn of the 20th century saw Vienna bestow the Secessionist style of art and architecture upon the world, a movement that became known outside the Austrian Empire as Art Nouveau.

World War I and World War II
Vienna experienced a difficult first half of the 20th century, with World War I leading to the collapse of the Habsburg Empire (the last emperor, Charles I, died in exile on Madeira in 1921) and a newly created Austrian Republic that

had to fend off attempts at a communist putsch, part of a period of political instability that was fuelled by the city's poor post-war economy.

Born in a small town on the Austrian border with Bavaria, Adolf Hitler had been an art student in Vienna before World War I, but left as a disillusioned and angry failure. Hitler returned in more triumphant circumstances in 1938, when he annexed Austria for the Third Reich, an act known as the Anschluss. The move was widely celebrated, with 200,000 people turning out on the Heldenplatz to cheer on the Führer. During World War II, Vienna's Jewish population faced severe persecution, and the vast majority were transported to concentration camps in Eastern Europe. Vienna suffered heavy damage from Allied bombing raids which targeted infrastructure and military sites. The city was liberated by Soviet forces in April 1945.

Vienna Today

Austria declared itself a neutral state in 1955, and the capital attracted large international bodies such as the United Nations, OPEC and the International Atomic Energy Agency. This neutrality

Tourists strolling along Graben in Vienna's beautiful old town

is often a problem for Austria's neighbours, as it puts the country on a different footing to the rest of Europe – for example, Austria is part of the EU but it refuses to join NATO. Since World War II, Vienna has become one of the most affluent and pleasant cities in Europe, attracting over eight million tourists a year. It is also one of the greenest capitals in the world, a fact that will no doubt stand it in good stead in decades to come.

Adolf Hitler announcing the annexation of Austria at the Heldenplatz

TOP 10
EXPERIENCES

Planning the perfect trip to Vienna? Whether you're visiting for the first time or making a return trip, there are some things you simply shouldn't miss out on. To make the most of your time – and to enjoy the very best this wonderfully varied city has to offer – be sure to add these experiences to your list.

1 Culture-crawl around the MuseumsQuartier

The MuseumsQuartier *(p42)* is one of the largest spaces for contemporary art and culture in the world. Cutting-edge modern design dazzles alongside Baroque architecture. Spend a day soaking up everything from fine art and fashion to theatre.

2 Enjoy the fun of the fair

Prater *(p71)* is home to Vienna's iconic ferris wheel, made famous by the film *The Third Man*. The amusement park features nostalgic rides alongside modern roller coasters. Afterwards, escape the hubbub and take a stroll through the surrounding park with its open meadows and shady trees.

3 Attend a classical music concert

Strauss, Mahler and Mozart provide the soundtrack to many people's expectations of Vienna. A concert at one of the country's oldest musical institutions, such as the Musikverein's Golden Hall *(p125)*, is an essential experience in the "City of Music".

4 Treat yourself to a Sachertorte

Ever wanted to try a dessert fit for royalty? The Sachertorte is a delicious cake invented for Prince Metternich at the Café Sacher *(p146)* in 1832. Head here to indulge in this chocolatey delight, layered with apricot jam, best served with a Viennese coffee.

5 Sip wine in a countryside tavern

Make the most of the vineyards surrounding Vienna by visiting a wine tavern in the city's wooded outskirts. Known as *Heurigen (p82)*, these rural retreats specialize in homegrown wine and traditional foods.

6 Shop at Vienna's largest market

The Naschmarkt *(p120)* is the city's most popular market, with over 100 stalls brimming with fresh produce, piles of dried fruit and an assortment of street food. Its Saturday flea market has become a cult event.

7 Marvel at the Hundertwasserhaus

A mosaic of colours and shapes, with undulating floors and plants spilling out from the rooftops, Friedensreich Hundertwasser's weird-and-wonderful apartment complex *(p48)* is one of Vienna's most famous façades.

8 Admire the U-Bahn's art

Not only is the U-Bahn *(p139)* the most efficient way to get around the city, it's also decorated with artwork. Lines U1, U2 and U3 include murals, sculptures and installations, while stations like Stadtpark flaunt Otto Wagner's mastery of Art Nouveau.

9 Explore the city by bike

Vienna is one of the world's most bike-friendly cities *(p141)*, so taking a bike for a spin should be at the top of your list. Cycle round the old city, taking in landmarks such as the Hofburg *(p26)*, or venture further out onto the Danube Cycle Path.

10 Dine at a Beisl

Homely and inviting, the traditional Viennese tavern, or Beisl, is the Austrian equivalent of a gastropub, offering hearty meals like schnitzel and strudel. Relax in the historic ambience of Griechenbeisl *(p67)*, one of the oldest restaurants in the city.

ITINERARIES

Exploring the MuseumsQuartier, tucking into Sachertorte, climbing up Stephansdom: there's a lot to see and do in Vienna. With places to eat, drink or simply take in the view, these itineraries offer ways to spend 2 days and 4 days in the city.

2 DAYS

Day 1

Morning

Kick-start your time in the Austrian capital at the Stephansplatz, Vienna's epicentre and its most famous square. This relatively small piazza is ringed with cafés and shops, and buzzes from dawn till late at night with tourists and locals going about their business. Almost filling the square is Vienna's top temple, the Gothic Stephansdom *(p22)*, St Stephen's Cathedral. Visitors can explore its catacombs and admire the beautiful interior packed with chapels, tombs and Gothic vaulting. The climb up the South Tower is an unmissable experience. For lunch, head into the surrounding tightly packed streets to a traditional Beisl (tavern) such as Griechenbeisl *(p67)* or Reinthaler's Beisl *(reinthalersbeisl.com)*.

> 📷 **VIEW**
> The panorama from the top of Stephansdom's South Tower is one of the city's best. The reward for climbing all 343 steps to get here: views of the church's ceramic roof, the Innere Stadt and beyond.

Afternoon

After lunch, head southwest out of the Innere Stadt and across the Burgring to the MuseumsQuartier *(p42)*, an entire neighbourhood of museums that was created from scratch two decades ago. This is one of the world's largest cultural complexes, blending period and modern architecture. Highlights include the Leopold Museum *(p42)*, containing works by Klimt and Schiele, the mumok *(p43)* museum of contemporary art and the Kunsthalle Wien *(p43)* exhibition space. With lots of hip cafés, shops and vibrant public spaces, this is a great place to hang out – and even stay for dinner at Café Leopold *(p43)*.

Stephansdom, with its imposing South Tower

Day 2

Morning

Skip your hotel breakfast in favour of a slice of Sachertorte and a coffee at Hotel Sacher *(p146)*, where Austria's most famous gateau was invented in 1832. From there, hotfoot it across the Burggarten to the Hofburg *(p26)*, former imperial residence of the Habsburg dynasty and now a complex of museums and cultural institutions. You could spend days exploring, but for now you'll need to limit yourself to a couple of sights. The Sisi Museum is a sure-fire winner, examining the life of arguable the most famous "first lady" of the Austrian Empire. Afterwards, grab a quick lunch at nearby Zum Alten Hofkeller cellar restaurant *(Schauflergasse 7)*.

Afternoon

After lunch, stay in the Hofburg to visit that most Viennese of attractions, the Spanish Riding School *(p30)*. Peek behind the scenes of the world's most famous horse attraction and learn all

A dress on display at the Sisi Museum in the Hofburg

about the stars of the show, the Lipizzaner steeds. Post tour, relax in the gardens of the Hofburg before heading for dinner at Plachutta *(p103)* for the best Viennese cuisine around.

EAT

Established in 1873, Café Landtmann is a renowned Viennese coffee house that's celebrated for its elegant old-world atmosphere, classic pastries and long list of historic patrons.

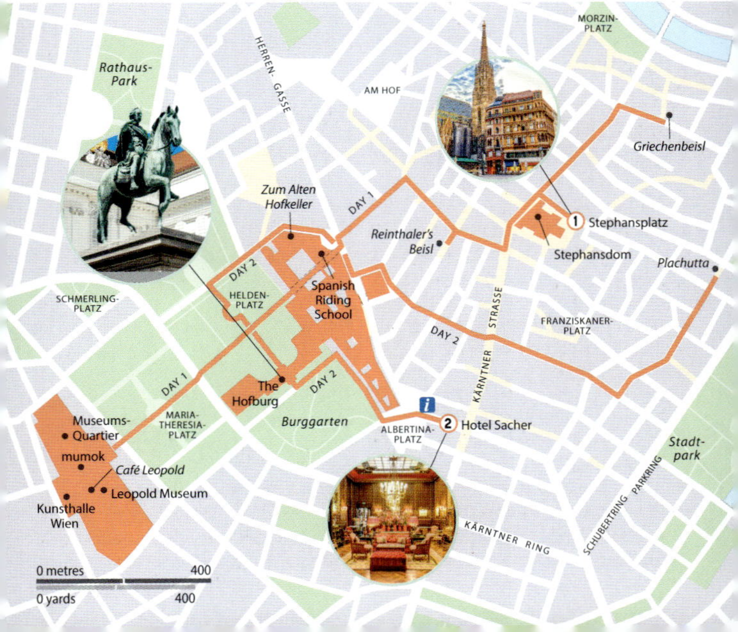

Map labels:

to Vienna Woods and Sirbu am Nussberg 7 km (4 miles)

TABORSTRASSE

DAY 2

U Praterstern

Prater

U Schwedenplatz

DAY 3 TAXI

Béla Béla

Buffet Trzesniewski

DAY 1

(1) Stephansdom

Käuzchen

Kunsthistorisches Museum

The Hofburg

Sofienwirt

Hundertwasser Village

Hundert-wasserhaus

LANDSTRASSER HAUPTSTRASSE

Museums-Quartier

DAY 2

i

Museums-Quartier

DAY 3

Stadtpark

DAY 4

4

DAY 4

Glacis Beisl

DAY 4

DAY 2

U Karlsplatz

Naschmarkt

(3)

Naschmarkt Deli

from Schönbrunn

0 metres   800
0 yards   800

Schloss Schönbrunn

Schloss Schönbrunn

Hollerei

(2)

U Schönbrunn

to Kunsthistorisches Museum

0 metres   900
0 yards   900

4 DAYS

Day 1

All roads in Vienna lead to the Stephansplatz, the city's old square, which is completely dominated by the Stephansdom (p22), Austria's most celebrated church. After visiting, grab a quick lunch at Buffet Trzesniewski (trzesniewski.at) of open sandwiches and a coffee (or beer). Dedicate the afternoon to the Hofburg (p26), the former imperial residence and one of the largest palace complexes in the world. There are so many museums and cultural institutions here, it's difficult to choose, but the Sisi Museum and the Imperial Apartments are two firm favourites. For dinner, Béla Béla (belabela.murmelz.com) near the Herrengasse metro station is a great choice for Mediterranean specialties.

> **TRANSPORT**
>
> Heurigen are located out in the Vienna Woods, so you'll need transport to reach them. By far the simplest option is to take an Uber, which avoids the need to work out byzantine timetables, especially on the return journey.

Day 2

Spend your morning touring the grand Baroque palace of Schloss Schönbrunn (p50), summer residence of the Austrian royal family; its opulent rooms are packed with treasures. Wander its gardens, then enjoy an inexpensive lunch at nearby Hollerei (hollerei.at).

The Kunsthistorisches Museum (p32), a short metro ride from Schönbrunn, is

EAT
There's a large concentration of restaurants and cafés around the Naschmarkt, with everything from Israeli, Korean, Chinese, Italian, Argentinian, Japanese and, of course, Viennese cuisine on offer.

one of Europe's top art museums, its walls lined with works by the biggest names in art history. A lively place for dinner afterwards is Käuzchen *(kaeuzchen.at)*, serving big platters of schnitzel and vegetarian fare.

Finish with a stroll in Prater *(p71)*, where you can enjoy a good old funfair with candy floss and bright lights.

Day 3

Today is all about food, starting at the city's top market, the Naschmarkt *(p120)*, where goodies of all kinds are stacked high on around 120 stalls. For a light lunch, try the Naschmarkt Deli *(naschmarktdeli.at)*, with its fusion of Mediterranean and Asian cuisines.

In the afternoon, take a taxi to the Vienna Woods *(p133)* for a relaxing stroll in the wooded hills and a visit to a traditional *Heurigen (p83)* such as Sirbu am Nussberg *(sirbu.at)*.

Day 4

Most museums fans will have been chomping at the bit to see the famous MuseumsQuartier *(p42)*, an entire district of the city centre given over to cultural spaces and events of all kinds. You really could spend all day here, but after lunch at nearby Glacis Beisl *(glacisbeisl.at)*, a traditional Viennese tavern, tear yourself away mid-afternoon to visit another piece of artistic Vienna, the unconventional Hundertwasserhaus *(p48)*, located across town in Kegelgasse. Its multi-coloured, iregular façade looks like a Picasso masterpiece. The building is inhabited and closed to the public, but nearby is the Hundertwasser Village *(hundertwasser-village.com)*, with shops and public spaces created by an artist in the Hundertwasser style. If you're still in the area come dinner-time, dine at Sofienwirt *(sofienwirt.at)*, which serves up a classic blend of Alpine and Mediterranean food.

A stall in the Naschmarkt, loaded with fresh produce

TOP 10 HIGHLIGHTS

Hundertwasserhaus

EXPLORE THE
HIGHLIGHTS

There are some sights in Vienna you simply shouldn't miss, and it's these attractions that make the Top 10. Discover what makes each one a must-see on the following pages.

HERRENGASSE

Volksgarten

HELDEN-PLATZ

BURGRING

MARIA THERESIEN-PLATZ

Burggarten

MUSEUMSTR.

GETREIDE MARKT

BABENBERGERSTRASSE

6

3

1 Stephansdom

2 The Hofburg

3 Kunsthistorisches Museum

4 The Belvedere

5 Karlskirche

6 MuseumsQuartier

7 Staatsoper

8 Secession Building

9 Hundertwasserhaus

10 Schloss Schönbrunn

0 metres	400
0 yards	400

WIPPLINGER STRASSE

Donaukanal

ROTENTURMSTRASSE

AM
HOF

INNERE
STADT

1

2

JOSEFS-
PLATZ

KÄRNTNER STRASSE

HIMMELPFORT-
GASSE

ALBERTINA-
PLATZ

7

SCHWARZENBERGSTR.

OPERNRING

ELISABETHSTR.

NIBELUNGENGASSE

8

AM
HEUMARKT

OPERNGASSE

Resselpark

WIEDNER HAUPTSTRASSE

KARLS-
PLATZ

RENNWEG

5

Belvedere
Garten

4

0 km   2
0 miles   2

HERNALS

Area of
main map

9

10

HIETZING

A22

A23

STEPHANSDOM

◉ N3 ⬚ St Stephen's Cathedral, Stephansplatz 3 ◷ 6am–10pm Mon–Sat, 7am–10pm Sun Ⓦ stephanskirche.at ▢▢

St Stephen's Cathedral is Vienna's most beloved landmark. Its foundations date back to 1147, but the earliest surviving features are the 13th-century Giant's Door and the Heathen Towers. The "Steffl", as the cathedral is called by the Viennese, suffered damage during World War II, but its rebuilding was seen as a symbol of hope.

1 Giant's Door
After a mammoth bone was found on the site during 15th-century construction works, the cathedral's main gate was renamed. It is decorated with beautiful sculptures that show Christ on Judgement Day between two angels.

2 Windows
The five medieval stained-glass windows behind the high altar relate biblical stories about the prophets and saints as well as the life and Passion of Jesus.

3 Vaulting
The Gothic main nave of the cathedral is covered by an impressive ribbed vault supported by tall pillars.

4 Pillars
The main nave of Stephansdom is dominated by soaring pillars, lavishly decorated with 77 clay and stone statues dating back to the 15th century.

5 North Tower and Pummerin
The North Tower, topped with a cupola, houses the huge Pummerin bell. Weighing 21 tonnes, this great bell was cast from 100 cannons seized during the failed siege of Vienna by the Turks in 1683. According to legend, construction of the North Tower, which begun in 1450, was never

TOP TIP

For great views, climb to the top of the South Tower or take the lift to the North Tower.

Richly decorated interior of the cathedral

completed because its master builder broke a pact he had made with the devil by speaking a holy name. As punishment, the devil caused the builder to fall to his death.

6 West Front
The two Romanesque Heathen Towers that flank the Giant's Door, and the two Gothic side chapels, with their filigree stone rose windows, make for a spectacular entry to the cathedral.

7 Organ
There has been an organ in the cathedral since 1334. The stunning west choir organ, with 125 stops and 10,000 pipes, was installed in the loft above the entrance in 1960.

8 High Altar
Stephansdom's beautiful Baroque high altar was created by the brothers Tobias and Johann Pock in 1647. The grand painting in the centre of the marble altar depicts the stoning of the cathedral's patron saint, St Stephen.

9 Tiled Roof
The impressive roof is covered with almost 230,000 colourful tiles laid out in the form of the Habsburg coat of arms, depicting a double-headed eagle wearing the emperor's crown and the Golden Fleece. Originally built before 1474, the roof was restored after fire damage in World War II.

10 Catacombs
When Charles VI closed the cathedral

Stephansdom Site Plan

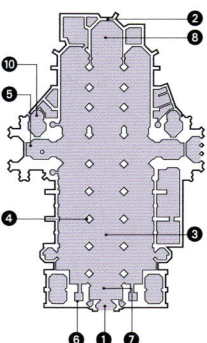

cemetery in 1732, vast catacombs were built below the cathedral to bury the city's dead. By the end of the 18th century, about 11,000 people were buried here. The Duke's Crypt has urns containing the internal organs of members of the Habsburg family.

Clockwise from right
Choir organ at the entrance to the chancel; intricately patterned tiled roof; Gothic façade of the cathedral

Gothic Features in the Cathedral

1. Master Pilgram
A self-portrait of Master Anton Pilgram – one of the key craftsmen that worked on the cathedral – can be seen at the base of the old organ.

2. Raised Tomb of Frederick III
Frederick III commissioned Niklas Gerhaert van Leyden to create a majestic raised tomb for him. It took 45 years to build and was finished 20 years after the emperor's death.

3. Baptismal Basin
Carved from red Salzburg marble, it took five years to finish this incredibly ornate 14-sided basin. Its decorations depict the seven holy sacraments, in the centre of which is Jesus's baptism.

4. Canopy with Pötscher Madonna
The 16th-century stone canopy shelters an icon of the Madonna from the Hungarian village of Máriapócs. In the 17th century, the story spread that tears ran down Mary's cheeks; today, people pray here for the sick.

5. Fenstergucker
In this marvellous example of the Viennese late Gothic period,

Fenstergucker, a self-portrait by Master Anton Pilgram

a sculpture of Master Pilgram himself leans out of an open window below the pulpit steps to inspect his own work.

6. Servants' Madonna
The graceful statue of the Madonna and Child is said to have miraculously helped acquit a maid who had been wrongly accused of stealing.

7. Pulpit
The lavishly decorated pulpit was created by Anton Pilgram in 1510. Lizards and toads, symbolizing evil, crawl up the balustrade, but are fought off by a dog, the symbol of good.

8. Cenotaph of Rudolf the Founder
Rudolf the Founder and his wife Katharina lie next to each other on their marble sarcophagus. The tomb was originally decorated with gold and precious jewels.

9. Wiener Neustädter Altar
The richly decorated altar just to the left of the main altar has four wings and shows 72 saints as well as scenes from the life of the Virgin Mary.

10. Gargoyles
The gargoyles on the exterior roof are made in the shape of dragons and other mythical animals to ward off evil.

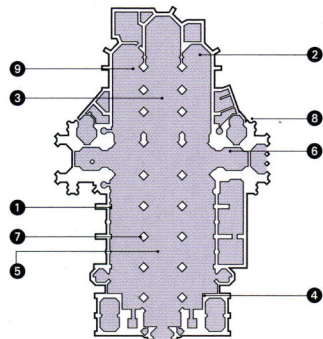

Stephansdom Site Plan

JOHANNES CAPISTRANUS AND THE TURKISH SIEGE

On the northeastern exterior wall of the cathedral is an elaborate Baroque pulpit cast in honour of the Italian Franciscan saint Giovanni di Capistrano (1385–1456), or Johannes Capistranus in German. Born in Italy, Johannes left a legal career after having a dream in which St Francis urged him to join the

Franciscan Order. He became a priest in 1425, and soon huge crowds flocked to hear him preach against heresy all over Italy. But it was for his peacemaking skills that he was best known. After missions in Italy and France, he was sent to Austria in 1451 to preach against the Turkish invasion, and he led the Christian army to victory against the Turks in the Siege of Belgrade in 1456. Johannes was canonized in 1724. Later that century, the limestone pulpit was erected in the Stephansdom; the 18th-century statue above it depicts the triumphant saint trampling a defeated Ottoman invader.

Statue of Capistranus on the pulpit

Funeral procession of Emperor Franz Joseph I in 1916

2

THE HOFBURG

📍 L4 🏛 Innerer Burghof/Kaisertor 🌐 sisimuseum-hofburg.at 🔗🔗

The Hofburg, Vienna's former imperial palace, is a lavish complex of buildings that houses, among other things, the offices of the Austrian president and the Spanish Riding School (p30). Originally a medieval castle, it was enlarged by successive Habsburg emperors up until 1918 – the Neue Burg (New Palace) is its most recent and grandest section.

1 Michaeler Gate
The majestic Michaeler Gate is the main entrance into the complex, and its green dome looms over Michaelerplatz.

2 Imperial Chapel
Although the original interior with carved statuary was altered by Maria Theresa, the Burgkapelle ("Castle Chapel") remains one of the oldest parts of the palace. Musicians including Mozart have given recitals here.

3 Austrian National Library
The Baroque library was built between 1723 and 1726 by Joseph Emanuel Fischer von Erlach. Adorned with ceiling frescoes, it houses a priceless collection of historic manuscripts in walnut bookcases.

4 Imperial Silver Collection
The elaborate serving bowl, table decorations and silverware in this collection show the splendour that marked meals at the imperial court.

TOP TIP

Book in advance for the Sunday choir at the Imperial Chapel, starting at 9:15am.

Ceiling frescoes in the Austrian National Library

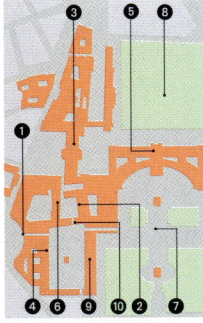

7 Heroes' Square
Prince Eugene of Savoy and Archduke Charles's equestrian statues dominate Heldenplatz (Heroes' Square), formerly a parade ground.

8 Burggarten and Volksgarten
Both of these pretty parks owe their origins to the Napoleonic troops who blew up parts of the palace in 1809, creating open spaces.

9 Imperial Apartments
🕐 9am–5:30pm daily (Jul & Aug: to 6pm)
The Kaiserappartements (imperial apartments) in the Amalia Wing are preserved as they were in the day of Franz Joseph I and his wife Elisabeth (p29). The six rooms dedicated to Elisabeth, or Sisi as she was affectionately known to Austrians, make up the Sisi Museum.

Grand exterior of the Hofburg

10 Swiss Gate
The name of this red-and-black Renaissance gate refers to the Swiss guards that were once employed by Empress Maria Theresa in the 18th century.

BUILDING THE PALACE

Each emperor left his mark on the palace until 1918. The Stallburg was built in the Renaissance under Maximilian II, while Amalienburg, constructed for his son Rudolf II, was completed in 1605. The oldest surviving part here is the Schweizertrakt (1552–3), featuring the Imperial Chapel and the Swiss Gate.

5 Museums
The semicircular Neue Burg, with its vast colonnaded façade, is home to collections of musical instruments, arms and armour, and the Weltmuseum Wien ethnological museum.

6 Secular and Ecclesiastical Treasuries
Magnificent artifacts are on display across 16 rooms dedicated to the relics of the Austrian and Holy Roman empires.

Admiring the silverware collection

Artistic Treasures in the Hofburg

1. Silverware and Porcelain
The *Silberkammer* displays the silverware and Vienna porcelain that was used for imperial banquets. This exhibit offers visitors a unique insight into courtly dining customs.

2. Musical Instruments
The impressive Sammlung Alter Musikinstrumente houses a collection of Renaissance and Baroque musical instruments, as well as pianos of Beethoven, Schubert and Haydn.

3. Imperial Orb and Sceptre
The enthroning of a new Habsburg ruler was accompanied by a ceremony of homage, during which the sovereign carried the orb and sceptre.

4. The Golden Fleece
This chainmail armour, made in 1517, consists of a neck chain and a collar of double-walled plates.

5. Austrian National Library Frescoes
Artist Daniel Gran painted these frescoes in the main hall in 1730 in honour of Emperor Charles VI. The statue here depicts the emperor as the centre of the universe, holding a balance between war and peace.

6. Captain Cook Artifacts
Among the exhibits in the Weltmuseum Wien ethnological museum are artifacts acquired by British explorer Captain James Cook on his voyages around the globe, including masks from North America.

7. Cradle of the King of Rome
This cradle was given by Marie Louise, Archduchess of Austria and second wife of Napoleon, to her son, the king of Rome. It is adorned with gold, silver and mother-of-pearl, while a goddess of victory crowns the child with a diadem of stars and a laurel wreath.

8. Aztec Feather Headpiece
The Penacho is the only one of its kind in existence today. Restoration of the 450 green quetzal tailfeathers and 1,000 gold plates was a joint project with Mexico.

9. Portrait of Empress Elisabeth
German painter and renowned court portraitist Franz Xaver Winterhalter painted this famous portrait of Empress Elisabeth in 1865. It hangs in one of the rooms of the Sisi Museum *(p27)*.

10. Crown of the Holy Roman Empire
Featured in the palace's collection of ecclesiastical and secular precious objects is this gold crown, decorated with gemstones and cloisonné enamel. It was crafted around 962 CE.

FRANZ JOSEPH AND SISI

Born in 1830, Franz Joseph was crowned emperor of Austria in 1848, aged 18. He met his wife, Princess Elisabeth of Bavaria, lovingly known to Austrians as "Sisi", in 1853 and they married shortly thereafter. The empress was adored by Austrians, then as now, for her extraordinary beauty, dignity and elegance in state matters. Many believed Franz Joseph's social successes were the result of Sisi's influence, and they considered her their "real" sovereign. The lives of the emperor and empress were not without trials and sorrows, however. Franz Joseph lost major wars to France (1848) and Prussia (1866), despite being crowned king of Hungary in 1867. They also suffered many personal tragedies – the emperor's brother, Maximilian, was executed in Mexico and his only son, Crown Prince Rudolf, committed suicide in 1889, after which Sisi only ever dressed in black. Austria, too, fell into mourning in 1898 when their beloved empress was assassinated in Geneva. Franz Joseph I ruled for 68 years, until his death in 1916.

Empress of Austria Elisabeth (1837–1898), also known as Sisi, at her coronation as queen of Hungary in 1867

Spanish Riding School

1. Horses' Steps
The steps of the famous white Lipizzaner stallions of the Spanish Riding School follow the rigid patterns of the "high art" of riding. Agility and strength are the goals. The most difficult part of the performance is the quadrille, which involves a precise and exact framework of choreography.

2. Emperor's Box
Once reserved for the imperial family, the Emperor's Box still offers the best seats in the house.

3. Lipizzaner Horses
The elegant white Lipizzaner stallions are bred at the national stud farm at Piber. The foals are born dark-skinned and acquire their trademark white coat between the ages of four and ten.

4. Training
The horses move from the stud farm to the Spanish Riding School when they are about four years old and are then trained for a minimum of eight years.

5. Portrait of Charles VI
A portrait of Charles VI riding on a white stallion hangs in the Royal Box. Riders entering the hall pay respect by raising their hats to the painting.

Horses and riders in perfect step, Winter Riding School

6. Winter Riding School
Since 1735, the Spanish Riding School has been located in the Winter Riding School building, designed by Austrian architect Johann Bernhard Fischer von Erlach in Baroque style.

7. Riders
Just like the horses, the riders at the school have to go through an extensive training period before they can perform classical dressage and other riding techniques. The riders traditionally wear white jodhpurs and a double-breasted, coffee-brown coat with brass buttons.

8. Stables
This Renaissance building in the Stallburg section of the Hofburg has an impressive three-storey gallery. It was built during the reign of Emperor Maximilian II.

9. Interior
The horses perform their elegant ballet in the 56-m- (180-ft-) long hall. The gallery here is supported by 46 Corinthian columns and decorated with elaborate plasterwork, chandeliers and a coffered ceiling.

10. Summer Riding School
During the summertime, performances and training sessions at the Spanish Riding School are carried out in a courtyard adjoining the Winter Riding School.

Portrait of Charles VI in the Royal Box

HISTORY OF THE LIPIZZANER HORSES

TOP 10
PIECES OF TACK
AND DRESS

1. Bicorn Napoleon hats
2. Brown cutaway tailcoats
3. Buckskin breeches
4. Knee-high black boots
5. Swan neck spurs
6. Buckskin saddles
7. Pale suede gloves
8. Gold-plated bridles
9. Saddlecloths (the colour indicates the rider's status)
10. Gold-plated horse breastplates

Maximilian II, Holy Roman Emperor

Spanish horses were first brought to Austria from Spain by the Holy Roman Emperor, Maximilian II (1527–76), in 1562, and the earliest evidence of them being housed in the Spanish Riding School dates back to 1572. In 1580, the horses were given the name Lipizzaner after a stud farm in Trieste; around this time, the first riding hall was built at the present location. Lipizzaner horses were originally produced by crossing Arab, Amizagh and Spanish horses, and are renowned for their grace and stamina. They begin learning the complex sequences of steps at the age of four. The school we know today was formed in the 19th century and hosted equestrian events where the horses performed in graceful formations. For 436 years, riders were exclusively male. In 2008, two women, one Austrian and the other British, were accepted into the school. Riding costumes have remained unchanged from the "Empire Style" of 1795.

Morning Exercise in the Hofreitschule, Josephsplatz by Julius von Blaas

3

KUNSTHISTORISCHES MUSEUM

⬚ K5 ⬚ Maria-Theresien-Platz ⬚ 10am–6pm Tue–Sun (to 9pm Thu)
⬚ khm.at 🔲🔲

Built in Italian Renaissance style by architects Karl von Hasenauer and Gottfried Semper, the Kunsthistorisches Museum was opened in 1891. It is a perfect setting for the artistic treasures assembled by the Habsburgs, who were enthusiastic patrons and collectors for centuries.

1 Maria Theresa's Breakfast Service

Crafted in Vienna around 1750, this pure-gold set belonged to the empress and consists of about 70 pieces. Some items, such as a mirror and a basin, are part of a washing set.

2 St Gregory with the Scribes

A late-9th-century ivory carving from Germany showing St Gregory and three scribes.

3 Summer

From 1562, Italian Giuseppe Arcimboldo served as portrait artist at the court of Rudolf II. He became famous for his heads composed of fruits and vegetables which served as allegorical representations. This one is from a set of four paintings that depict the four seasons of the year.

***Summer* (1563) by Giuseppe Arcimboldo**

4 Blue Hippo

Hippo figurines are often found in the tombs of Ancient Egypt, as they were thought to help gain entry into the afterlife. This one has drawings of plants from the Nile Delta on its body.

5 Stela of Ha-hat, Thebes

The stela (stone slab), which is more than 2,500 years old, is lavishly painted in gold, red and blue and depicts Osiris among other Egyptian gods, who are praised in the

Kunsthistorisches Museum Floorplan

Key to Floorplan
▢ First floor
▢ Ground floor

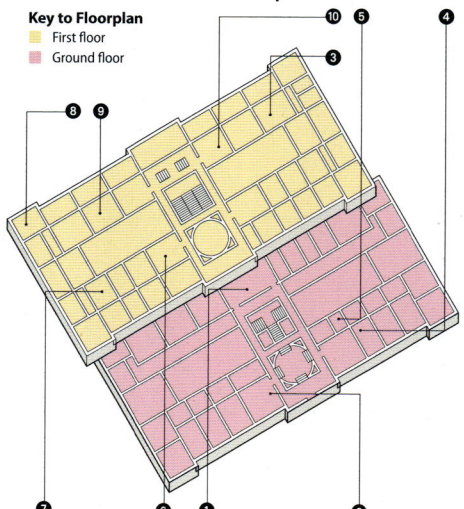

Browsing Renaissance paintings in the museum

inscriptions. The stela was discovered inside a tomb in Thebes.

6 Large Self-Portrait

The Dutch master artist Rembrandt painted this canvas in 1652, depicting everything around him in dark colours, with his face the only area of light.

7 The Fur

This 1638 painting is the most intimate portrait of Peter Paul Rubens's wife Hélène, whom he married

Peasant Wedding by Pieter Bruegel the Elder

late in life and whose features he often incorporated into his works. In a naturally graceful pose, the young woman evokes Venus, the Roman goddess of love.

8 Virgin and Child with a Pear

German artist Albrecht Dürer (1471–1528) painted many Madonna pictures, but this one is among the best known. It shows the Virgin Mary bending over a child (believed to be Jesus) holding a pear core.

9 Peasant Wedding

More than any of his other works, this 1568 painting contributed to Pieter Bruegel the Elder's fame as a portrayer of peasant life. The viewer feels right in the middle of a rustic wedding.

10 Madonna of the Cherries

A number of paintings by Titian can be found in the Italian Collection. In this one (1518), the Madonna's dress is painted in the red-brown colours for which the artist is known.

 MUSEUM GUIDE

On the ground floor, the right wing houses the Egyptian Collection and Greek and Roman Antiquities, while the left wing is home to the Kunsthammer (Chamber of Art and Wonders). The stairs to the first floor lead to the Picture Gallery. The second floor has the Coin Cabinet and Vermeyen cartoons.

The Kunsthistorisches' Collections

1. Egyptian Collection
This section has a remarkably extensive stock of pieces from the Old and Middle Kingdoms of Ancient Egypt. The collection was amassed in the 19th and 20th centuries, developed by purchases, donations and new acquisitions from excavations.

2. Greek and Roman Antiquities
The collection, originating from the former estate of the Habsburgs, covers a period of history extending from 3rd-century-BCE Cypriot Bronze Age pottery to Slavic finds from the beginning of the 1st century CE. It is also internationally renowned as the home of the unique cameos and archaeological treasures dating from the Great Migration and the Early Middle Ages.

3. Kunstkammer (Chamber of Art and Wonders)
Completely redesigned in 2013, this magnificent collection was amassed by emperors and archdukes in the Renaissance and Baroque periods. The Kunstkammer has 20 galleries

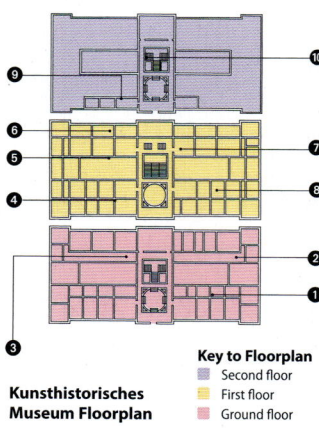

Kunsthistorisches Museum Floorplan

Key to Floorplan
- Second floor
- First floor
- Ground floor

and 2,200 pieces, and is justifiably known as "a museum within a museum". Natural objects thought to have magical powers vie with masterpieces such as Maria Theresa's breakfast service *(p32)* and the celebrated *Saliera* (saltcellar) by Benvenuto Cellini.

4. German Collection
This collection has many 16th-century paintings. Among them are works by Dürer, Cranach the Elder and Holbein the Younger.

5. Flemish Collection
A great number of works from 17th-century Flanders made their way into the museum because of Habsburg family ties to this part of Europe. The highlights are works by Rubens and Jan van Eyck.

6. Dutch Collection
This section (15th to 17th century) includes a collection of works by Pieter Bruegel the Elder, containing about a third of all his surviving pictures.

7. Italian Collection
The majority of the 15th- to 18th-century Italian paintings were collected by Archduke Leopold

Jane Seymour, Queen of England **(1536) by Hans Holbein the Younger**

Wilhelm, who founded the collection in the 17th century. They are mainly from the Venetian Renaissance period of the late 15th to late 16th centuries, with major works by Titian, Veronese, Canaletto and Tintoretto.

8. Spanish and French Collection

Thanks to Habsburg connections, portraits of the Spanish royal family form part of this collection. Diego Velázquez's portraits of the Infanta Margarita Teresa (daughter of Philip IV of Spain) are on display.

9. Coin Cabinet

There are more than 700,000 objects, including coins, paper money, medals and banknotes from three millennia on display in this fascinating numismatic collection.

10. The Vermeyen Cartoons

These large cartoons, or sketches, depict various scenes from Emperor Charles V's Tunis campaign of 1535. They were produced by court painter

The Conquest and Pillage of Tunis **(c 1545) by Jan Cornelisz Vermeyen**

Jan Cornelisz Vermeyen (who accompanied the emperor on the campaign). Willem de Pannemaker used them as models for 12 tapestries that now hang in the Palacio Real (Royal Palace) in Madrid.

Displays in the museum's Coin Cabinet collection

THE BELVEDERE

F5–G6 Prinz-Eugen-Strasse 27 belvedere.at

Prince Eugene of Savoy commissioned the two Belvedere palaces with money he had received as a reward for his victories during the War of the Spanish Succession. The payment allowed him to carry out one of the most ambitious building projects ever undertaken by a private individual. The palaces were built by Johann Lukas von Hildebrandt in 1714–23 as the prince's summer residence.

1 Upper Belvedere
G6 9am–6pm daily

Built to impress, and never inhabited, this elaborate palace houses the greatest collection of Austrian art in the world, dating from medieval times to today.

2 Marble Hall
The most beautiful room within the Upper Belvedere, the Marble Hall has a lavish frescoed ceiling. The Austrian State Treaty was signed here in 1955.

TOP TIP
It is advisable to book a time slot to visit the Upper and Lower Belvederes.

3 Sala Terrena
Located on the ground floor, beneath the Marble Hall, is the stunning Sala Terrena hall, with four massive statues supporting the stunning vaulted ceiling. White stuccowork covers the walls and ceiling of the hall.

4 French Gardens
The Baroque gardens and terraces include the private flowers of Prince Eugene and Europe's oldest alpine gardens.

5 Garden Statues
Of the numerous statues dotted around the gardens, the Eight Muses and the Sphinxes are the most outstanding.

6 Lower Belvedere
F5 Rennweg 6 10am–6pm daily

The opulent Baroque palace, set in beautiful

Clockwise from right **Impressive interior of the Sala Terrena; one of the many marble statues in the pretty Belvedere gardens; ornate ceiling of the Marble Hall**

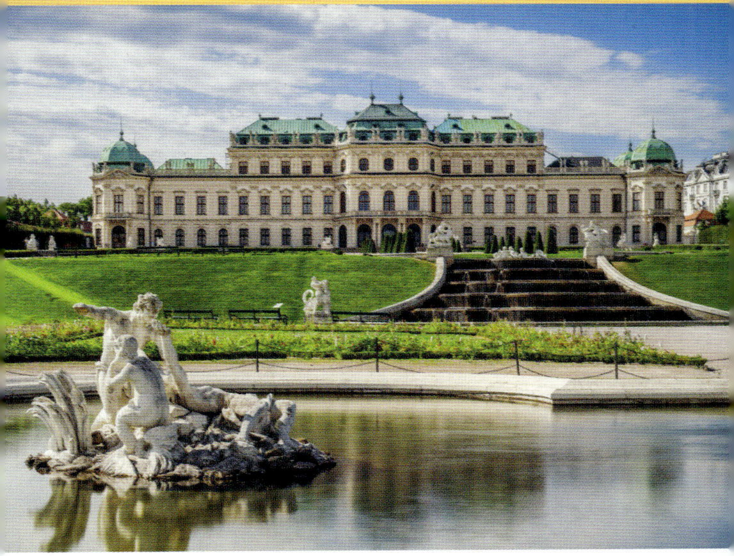

Upper Belvedere complex and its immaculate gardens

Key to Floorplan

Upper Belvedere

Lower Belvedere

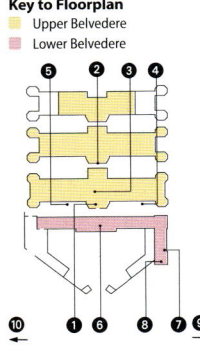

The Belvedere Floorplan

landscaped gardens, was the former living quarters and state rooms of Prince Eugene. It now houses special exhibitions only.

7 Marble Gallery

Constructed with niches to hold classical statues, this grandiose room has a stucco ceiling showing a heroic Prince Eugene being honoured.

8 Gold Cabinet

A statue of Prince Eugene of Savoy stands in this Lower Belvedere room. The walls of this room are entirely covered by huge gilt-framed mirrors.

9 Orangery and Palace Stables

Adjacent to the Lower Belvedere, the Orangery is a modern, white exhibition space. The Stables feature examples of different painting styles.

10 Belvedere 21

H6 Quartier Belvedere, Arsenalstrasse 1 11am–6pm Tue–Sun (to 9pm Thu)

This Modernist building was Austria's pavilion for Expo 58 (Brussels' World Fair in 1958). It was moved to Vienna and is now a museum of contemporary art. It also has an interesting cinema and workshop programme.

SIGNING THE STATE TREATY

In May 1955, the Upper Belvedere was the scene of much rejoicing when the Austrian State Treaty was signed by the four Allied powers that had occupied Austria since the end of World War II, ten years earlier. In the Marble Hall, John Foster Dulles (US), Vyacheslav Molotov (USSR), Harold Macmillan (UK) and Antoine Pinay (France) put their signatures to the document granting sovereignty to Austria once more. The treaty was then displayed from the hall's balcony to the cheering crowds below.

Artworks in the Belvedere

1. Napoleon at the Saint Bernard Pass
Jacques-Louis David's idealized rendering of Napoleon (1803) depicts him crossing the Alps into Italy in 1801 on a white stallion. In fact, Bonaparte made this journey on a mule.

2. Still Life with Dead Lamb
Seen as a metaphor for a world that's lost its way, this still life (1910) is one of Oskar Kokoschka's most notable works.

3. Adolescentia
Elena Luksch-Makowsky was the first female member of the Vienna Secession. Her painting *Adolescentia* (1903), depicting the transition from childhood to adulthood, is a striking example of the Secessionist style.

4. Character Heads
Franz Xaver Messerschmidt was one of the most eccentric artists of the 18th century. His "Character Heads" (1770–83) series presents busts with extreme facial expressions.

5. The Chef
This 1882 portrait (also known as *Le Père Paul*) by Claude Monet shows the

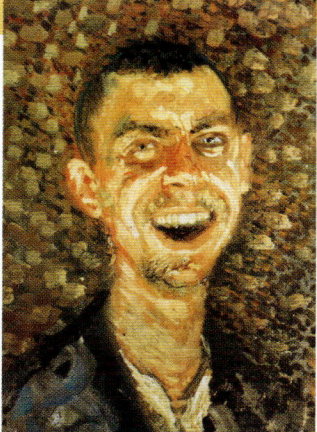

Richard Gerstl's
Self-Portrait, Laughing

renowned chef Paul Antoine Graff, who owned a small hotel on the Normandy coast at which Monet stayed.

6. Self-Portrait, Laughing
Painted the same year that he committed suicide (1908), Richard Gerstl tries one last attempt at defiant self-definition.

7. Znaimer Altarpiece
The carved inner sides of this magnificent triptych (c 1427) depict the events of Good Friday as recorded in the Gospel of St Matthew.

8. The Kiss
Painted in 1909, Gustav Klimt's most celebrated work, *The Kiss*, features the linear style and organic forms that characterize the Secessionists' work.

9. Death and the Maiden
A man and a woman are clutching each other on a sheet spread over uneven terrain in this painting (1915). Artist Egon Schiele painted his own features on the man.

10. Farmhouse in Upper Austria
Although Klimt is known for his figure paintings, landscapes also played a key part in his work. From 1900, he spent most summers in Salzkammergut, painting scenes such as this (1911).

The Belvedere Floorplan

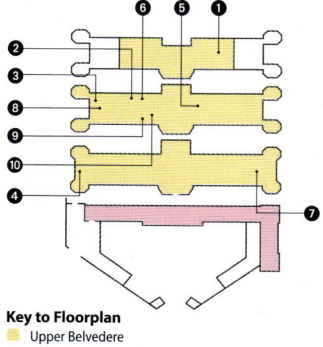

Key to Floorplan
Upper Belvedere
Lower Belvedere

THE SECESSIONIST MOVEMENT

Klimt's famous artwork, *The Kiss*

Formed in 1897, the Secessionist style was a reaction against the conservative "historicism" of the Association of Austrian Artists, Vienna's dominant artistic union, which continues to flourish and today occupies the Albertina Modern *(p65)*. The leader and first president of the breakaway Union of Austrian Artists was Gustav Klimt. Members included Koloman Moser, Josef Hoffmann, Max Kurzweil, Elena Luksch-Makowsky and Wilhelm Bernatzik. Architect Otto Wagner joined later. The group was called the "Vienna Secession", as their movement followed similar rebellions in Berlin and Munich. Secessionism has no single defining stylistic theme, aside from the desire to eliminate historical influences. Its masterpiece is the Secession Building *(p46)*, which serves as a popular exhibition hall for contemporary art.

Members of the Vienna Secession at an exhibition in 1902

KARLSKIRCHE

F4 · Karlsplatz · 7:30am–7pm Mon–Sat, 9am–7pm Sun
karlskirche.at

St Charles's Church was built between 1715 and 1737 to honour Karl Borromeo, patron saint of the fight against the plague. The aim was to thank God for delivering Vienna from the epidemic in 1713. Designed by Johann Fischer von Erlach, this architectural masterpiece borrows from classical Greek and Roman Baroque architecture.

TOP TIP

To access the narrow panorama viewpoint, visitors have to climb 167 steps.

1 Entrance
The stunning façade is winged by two gatehouses that are built in a style similar to that of Chinese pavilions and lead into the side entrances. At the centre of the façade is the stairway, atop which is a Classical pediment supported by six pillars.

2 Columns
Inspired by the ancient Roman Trajan's Column, the church's two huge columns depict scenes from the life of St Karl Borromeo. The left column shows the quality of steadfastness, while the column on the right shows courage.

3 Cupola with Frescoes
The fresco by Johann Michael Rottmayr on the interior of the dome depicts the Virgin Mary begging the Holy Trinity to deliver the population from the plague.

Cupola fresco by Johann Michael Rottmayr

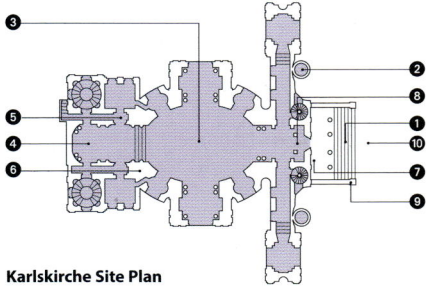

Karlskirche Site Plan

Baroque façade of Karlskirche

JOHANN FISCHER VON ERLACH

Many of Vienna's finest buildings were designed by Johann Fischer von Erlach (1656–1723). The Graz-born architect studied in Rome, and then moved to Vienna, where he became a leading exponent of the Baroque style. After Erlach's death in Vienna, Karlskirche was completed by his son.

4 High Altar

The high altar, designed in typical Baroque style, was probably planned by Fischer von Erlach himself. It features a stucco relief by Albert Camesina illustrating St Karl Borromeo being carried into heaven on a cloud laden with angels and cherubs.

5 Altar Paintings

The side altars feature several paintings, but the most remarkable are those by master artist Daniel Gran. His most famous paintings, including *The Healing of a Gout Victim*, *Jesus and the Roman Captain* and *Saint Elisabeth of Hungary*, can be found in the church.

6 Pulpit

Atop the church's richly gilded pulpit are two cherubs on the canopy, and it is decorated with *rocailles* (scrolls) and garlands of flowers.

7 Pediment Reliefs

The pediment resembles the covering of a Greek temple. Its artful reliefs show the suffering of the Viennese during the 1713 plague.

8 Karl Borromeo Statue

Designed by Lorenzo Mattielli, this statue of the patron saint of the fight against the plague sits on the church's pediment.

9 Angels

Statues of two angels guard the exterior stairway. The angel on the right represents the New Testament; the one on the left, the Old Testament.

10 Pond with Henry Moore Sculpture

In front of the church lies a stone-paved pond, atop which rests a bronze Henry Moore sculpture. The modern figure contrasts sharply with the Baroque style of the church.

Statue of an angel holding a cross in the Karlskirche

6

MUSEUMSQUARTIER

J5 ⌂ Museumsplatz 1 ⓦ mqw.at

One of Europe's most vibrant cultural complexes, the Museum Quarter (or MQ) has a fascinating history. Its first buildings, commissioned by Charles VI in 1713, were imperial stables designed by Johann Fischer von Erlach and completed in 1725. In 1918, the complex was transformed into an exhibition ground. Today, the MQ is home to over 70 cultural centres, along with numerous shops and restaurants.

1 Dschungel
4:30–6:30pm Mon–Fri ⓦ dschungel wien.at
This theatre hub for kids and families features puppets, dance, film and opera in two auditoriums.

2 Leopold Museum
10am–6pm Wed–Mon ⓦ leopold museum.org
The museum houses an outstanding array of modern Austrian art. It has the world's biggest Egon Schiele collection (over 40 paintings and 180 drawings), as well as paintings by Klimt.

TOP TIP

The Leopold Museum shop has lovely art-themed souvenirs for sale.

3 Tanzquartier Wien
9am–7.30pm Mon–Fri, 10am–7:30pm Sat ⓦ tqw.at
Known as TQW, this performance and study venue focuses solely on modern dance.

4 wienXtra-kinderinfo
Hours vary, check website ⓦ wienxtra.at
WienXtra has a play area for kids under 13 and an

Courtyard of the MuseumsQuartier

Exhibition at the Leopold Museum

> **EAT**
> Modern Café Leopold *(cafeleopold.wien)*, in the Leopold Museum, offers an Asian-inspired menu. Breakfast deals also include entry to the museum.

information centre offering free advice on kids' activities in Vienna.

5 ZOOM
🕐 Hours vary, chech website 🌐 kinder museum.at
An exciting place for kids aged eight months to 14 years, ZOOM offers interactive learning using a wide range of fun-filled activities and exhibitions.

6 Q21
🕐 10am–6pm daily (to 9pm Thu) 🌐 mqw.at
Vienna's centre for contemporary applied art, Q21 stages numerous creative initiatives that are spread all over the MQ. Street art and daily exhibitions, as well as office and editing spaces for

the artists in residence, are among its many programmes.

7 Halle E+G
🕐 10am–1pm & 2–7pm Mon–Sat 🌐 halleneg.at
These two event halls host music, dance and musical theatre performances. The Baroque Halle E once housed horses.

8 Kunsthalle
🕐 10am–6pm Tue–Sun (to 9pm Thu) 🌐 kunsthalle wien.at 🔗
Considered the latest outpost of the contemporary art exhibition space, Kunsthalle hosts frequently changing exhibitions featuring up-and-coming artists.

It has two venues, one on MuseumsQuartier and another one on Karlsplatz *(p65)*.

9 mumok
🕐 10am–6pm Tue–Sun 🌐 mumok.at 🔗
This grey basalt lava building is home to a collection of 20th-century masterpieces.

10 Az W
🕐 10am–7pm daily 🌐 azw.at 🔗
The Austrian Architecture Museum features exhibits, regular lectures and an extensive academic library.

Exploring the exhibits at ZOOM

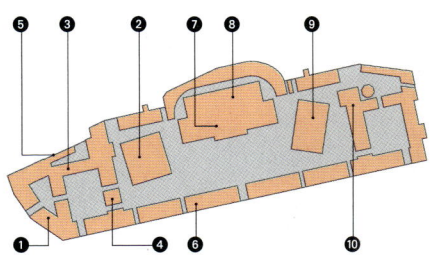

MuseumsQuartier Site Plan

7

STAATSOPER

M5 ☐ Opernring 2 ☐ For guided tours; hours vary, check website
☐ wiener-staatsoper.at ☐ ☐

Designed by Eduard van der Nüll and August von Siccardsburg, the Neo-Renaissance State Opera House opened in May 1869. With its exceptional accoustics, the lavish auditorium is surely the finest performance space in the city, playing host to a vibrant programme of over 350 performances each season.

1 Exterior
Seen from the Ringstrasse, the majestic pale stone building is dominated by the original loggia, which survived World War II.

2 Bronze Statues
The large bronze statues, placed in the five arches of the loggia, are the creation of Ernst Julius Hähnel (1876) and are allegories of heroism, drama, fantasy, comedy and love, as seen from left to right.

3 Tea Salon
The sumptuous Tea Salon is one of the most splendid rooms in the building. Its centre-piece is a fireplace flanked by pillars and mirrors.

4 Reliefs of Opera and Ballet
Created by Johann Preleuthner, two reliefs show the two art forms performed in the house: opera and ballet.

5 Grand Staircase
The magnificent marble staircase, decorated with frescoes, mirrors and chandeliers, leads to the auditorium. Its arches are embellished with statues by Josef Gasser, depicting the seven liberal arts: architecture, poetry, dance, sculpture, art, music and drama.

6 Auditorium
Following its destruction in World War II, it was decided, after much discussion, that the auditorium be rebuilt to its original 1869 design with three box circles and two open circles. The centrepiece is a huge 3,000-kg (6,600-lb) crystal chandelier.

Performance stage in the auditorium

TOP TIP

Standing-room-only tickets (€13–18) go on sale 80 minutes before curtain up.

Grand staircase surrounded by statues

VIENNA
OPERA BALL

The highlight of Vienna's social calendar is the annual Opera Ball, held on the last Thursday of the *Fasching* (carnival season) in the Staatsoper. This event is attended by 5,000 people, including international celebrities. Seats in the audito-rium make way for a dance floor where guests waltz the night away. The first postwar dance was held in 1956, after the country had started to recover from years of occupation.

7 Schwind Foyer

In the superb Schwind Foyer are 16 oil paintings by Moritz von Schwind. They represent some famous operas, including Rossini's *The Barber of Seville* (1816) and Beethoven's *Fidelio* (1805). A bust of each composer is placed beneath each illustration.

8 Gustav Mahler Bust

The bronze bust of world-renowned composer Gustav Mahler, who served as director of the Vienna Court Opera from 1897 to 1907, was created by Auguste Rodin in 1909. It is placed in the Schwind Foyer alongside busts of other "conducting directors" of the opera.

9 Tapestries

Nine tapestries in the Gustav Mahler Hall, designed by Vienna-based Austrian artist Rudolf Eisenmenger (1902–94), show scenes from Mozart's opera *The Magic Flute*.

10 Fountains

The two imposing fountains that can be seen on the right and left sides of the opera house were created by the famed Austrian sculptor Josef Gasser (1817–68). They represent two different worlds: music, dance, joy and levity on the left, and the siren Lorelei with love, revenge and sorrow, on the right.

Staatsoper as seen from the Albertina

8

SECESSION BUILDING

L6 ⬥ Friedrichstrasse 12 ⬥ 10am–6pm Tue–Sun ⬥ secession.at ⬥

The large, white, cubic Secession Building was designed in 1897 by Joseph Maria Olbrich, the Austrian architect and co-founder of the Vienna Secession, as the manifesto of the late-19th-century art movement. When first unveiled, the radical building was derided by the public; today, it is one of the most treasured examples of a particularly Viennese artistic period.

Façade of the Secession Building

1 Façade
Due to its huge, unbroken walls, the building appears to be constructed from solid cubes.

2 Architecture
The ground plan of the pavilion reveals simple geometrical forms, taking the square as the basic shape. The framework is softened by curves and ornaments.

3 Motto
Above the entrance of the pavilion is the gold motto of the Secessionist movement *"Der Zeit ihre Kunst. Der Kunst ihre Freiheit"* – "To every age its art, to art its freedom."

4 Gorgon Heads
The entrance is decorated with the heads

> ☕ **DRINK**
> Grab a drink and something to eat at the trendy wine shop Wien & Co Bar *(wienco.at)* across from the Secession Building.

of the three Gorgons, which represent architecture, sculpture and painting. The sides also feature owls, which, with the Gorgons, are virtues of Pallas Athena, Greek goddess of wisdom, victory and the crafts.

Heads of the three Gorgons, at the entrance

5 Ornaments
The building is decorated with gilt laurel garlands, floral patterns and plants along the sides of the walls. Most striking is the gold tree above the main door.

6 Flowerpots
The blue mosaic flowerpots on either side of the entrance door are carried by four turtles. Their small trees add a touch of nature to the building's hard lines.

7 Dome
Made of 2,500 gilt laurel leaves and 311 berries, the dome is the most prominent feature of the design. The laurel symbolizes victory, dignity and purity.

8 Interior
The exhibition hall, in the shape of a basilica with a lofty nave and two lower aisles, can be easily adapted for each show staged here. Almost completely covered by a glass roof, by day it's bathed in a constant and even light.

9 Beethoven Frieze
Created by Gustav Klimt in 1902 for an exhibition paying homage to Ludwig van Beethoven, the 34-m- (110-ft-) long masterpiece of Viennese Art Nouveau tells a story of the composer's Ninth Symphony, *Ode to Joy*.

10 Mark Anthony Statue
The bronze sculpture of the Roman general Mark Anthony in a chariot drawn by lions was created by Arthur Strasser in 1898. It was displayed at the fourth exhibition in the Secession and then set outside the building.

THE FEMALE SECESSION

Russian-born Elena Luksch-Makowsky (1878–1967) was the first female member of the Vienna Secession *(p39)*. Her work often centreed on her experiences as an artist and mother, drawing on elements of the Secession movement and her Russian upbringing. Her famous pieces include *Ver Sacrum* (1901) and *Adolescentia (p38)*.

Gustav Klimt's masterpiece
Beethoven Friez

9

HUNDERTWASSERHAUS

🏠 Kegelgasse 36–38 🌐 hundertwasser-haus.info

Opened in March 1986, this fairytale house with onion spires, a green roof and multicoloured façade is one of the city's most visited landmarks. Flamboyant Austrian artist Friedensreich Hundertwasser designed it as a playful take on usually dull social housing to show that practical could also be beautiful. Today, almost 200 people live in the 50 apartments.

1 Façade
The unusual curving irregularity of this building is an expression of sheer architectural exuberance. The front of the house is painted in bright shades of red, blue, yellow and white, and each of the differently coloured sections marks one apartment. The many trees growing in the rooftop gardens of the apartment block are also very unusual.

2 Main Entrance
The building's main entrance, situated on Löwengasse, is an open section leading to the inner courtyard of the building. The apartments set just above the main entrance are supported by colourful pillars. In front of the entrance is an attractive small fountain where visitors can sit and relax.

3 Onion Towers
Two stunning golden onion towers stand out amid the traditional city skyline, gleaming atop the Hundertwasserhaus. These remarkable towers are a striking feature of the apartment's distinctive design.

4 Roof Gardens
Roof gardens on the multilevel block are a key feature of the building's design. Each apartment has access to a little piece of nature in the form

Main entrance to the apartment block

TOP TIP

The apartments are private residences and can be viewed only from outside.

Roof gardens on the multilevel block

FRIEDENSREICH HUNDERTWASSER

When Friedensreich Hundertwasser (1928–2000) left the Vienna Academy of Fine Arts in 1948 after only three months of study, it was hard to imagine that he would one day become one of Austria's most acclaimed artists and a master of design. Bright colours contrasted by black and gold, and the spiral, which he used in his work gradually became his artistic trademarks. Hundertwasser's aim was to create architecture in harmony with nature and humankind.

of the roof gardens and balconies that are scattered all over the building. The gardens have some 250 large trees, trimmed shrubs and a grass lawn.

5 Irregular Windows

Hundertwasser believed that windows constitute a house's soul, so all the windows here vary in size and shape, and each of them is framed by a complementary colour.

6 Ceramic Line

The size of every apartment is visible as it's marked by an uneven line of ceramic tiles giving a kaleidoscopic effect.

7 Decorations

The building is decorated with black, white and golden tiles. Statues on the corners of balconies, painted animals and plants on the corridor walls, and roof gardens give the place a lovely, cheerful appearance.

8 Glass Front

The two towers of the house – those crowned by the onion domes – host the central staircase. Thanks to the glass fronts, by day they are always light and airy.

9 Pillars

A prominent feature of the structure is the range of brightly coloured, irregularly shaped shiny pillars. Some of these pillars are integrated in the building and function as mere decoration, while others are more practical and are used to support the gallery that runs along the first floor of the block.

10 Pavement

The area around Löwengasse is pedestrianized with some relaxed seating spots and elegant lampposts. Visitors can explore the nearby shops and cafés.

One of the colourful pillars supporting the building

SCHLOSS SCHÖNBRUNN

⬛ H1 🏛 Schönbrunner Schloss Strasse 47 ⏰ Hours vary, chech website
🌐 schoenbrunn.at 🚻 📷

The former summer residence of the Habsburgs, Schönbrunn Palace was built between 1695 and 1713 to the designs of Johann Fischer von Erlach. Little of his original plans remain – Empress Maria Theresa ordered most of the interior to be redesigned in Rococo style. The façade was altered in 1817–19, when it was painted in the characteristic "Schönbrunn yellow".

Schloss Schönbrunn Site Plan

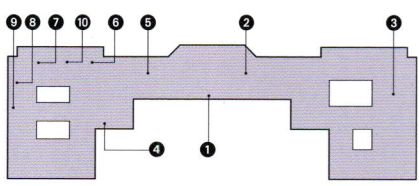

room, there are portraits of Emperor Joseph I as a child and his famous sister Marie Antoinette.

1 Grand Gallery
This 40-m- (130-ft-) long, 10-m- (30-ft-) wide gallery has a stunning Rococo design of tall windows, splendid crystal mirrors, chandeliers and white-and-gold stucco. The gallery is still used for state receptions and banquets.

2 Porcelain Room
Maria Theresa's former study walls are covered with carved wooden frames painted blue and white.

3 Empress Elisabeth Salon
In Empress Elisabeth's Neo-Rococo reception

4 Chapel
In 1740, Maria Theresa remodelled the chapel. The marble altar was designed by Georg Raphael Donner, and

> **TOP TIP**
>
> At the on-site Children's Museum, kids can dress up as Habsburgs.

PALACE GUIDE

Head to the left wing from the main gate, where you can buy tickets to visit the interior and pick up a map. To the right of the palace are the gardens (*p52*), home to the Wagenburg and Palemhaus. Behind the palace are lovely Baroque-style flowerbeds.

Paul Troger painted the ceiling fresco *The Marriage of the Virgin*.

5 Bergl Rooms

The garden rooms were painted with frescoes by Johann Wenzel Bergl (1768–77) to satisfy Maria Theresa's taste for enchanting landscapes.

6 Blue Chinese Salon

Decorated with Chinese paper wall hangings, this salon was once the council chamber of Emperor Franz I Stephan.

7 Napoleon's Room

When Napoleon occupied Vienna in 1805 and 1809 he made the Schloss Schönbrunn his headquarters and stayed in this splendid room. Beautiful Flemish tapestries from the 18th century adorn the walls.

8 Millions' Room

The name derives from the room's rosewood panelling, which cost a reputed one million Gulden (former Austrian gold coins). In the exquisite wall panels, Indo-Persian watercolour miniatures illustrate scenes from the lives of the Mughal rulers of India in the 16th and 17th centuries.

9 Mirror Room

With magnificent gilt white-and-gold Rococo decoration, wooden panelling and crystal mirrors, this room is a fine example of Maria Theresa's style.

The stunning Schloss Schönbrunn

Mozart once gave a private performance for the empress here.

10 Vieux-Laque Room

This room unites Rococo elements with Chinese art: the impressive black lacquer panels show landscapes adorned in gold. After her husband Francis I died in 1765, Maria Theresa hung portraits of him here as a memorial.

Black lacquer panels in the Vieux-Laque Room

Features of Schönbrunn's Gardens

1. Schlosstheater
Commissioned by Maria Theresa, the theatre opened in 1747. The empress and her many children performed on the stage as singers.

2. Palmenhaus
The stunning steel-and-glass palm house was built in 1881–2 by Franz Xaver Segenschmid, using the latest technology. The central pavilion is 28-m (90-ft) high and has two wings.

Ornate ceremonial state coach at Wagenburg

3. Beautiful Fountain
A fresh spring was discovered by Emperor Matthias while hunting in the area in 1619. In 1630, a well, together with a statue of a Roman nymph, was placed here, and it gave the palace its name (Schönbrunn is German for "beautiful fountain"). The fountain is close to the Roman Ruins.

4. Roman Ruins
Built in 1778, the Roman Ruins were designed to enhance the prestige of the Habsburgs by presenting them as the successors to the Roman emperors.

5. Wagenburg
A highlight of the Wagenburg (carriage museum) is the richly decorated imperial coach, which was built for the coronation of Joseph II in 1765.

6. Gloriette
At the summit of the park's hill is the Gloriette, its most prominent feature. The arcaded edifice, designed by Johann Ferdinand Hetzendorf von Hohenberg, was once used as a dining hall before it became a viewing point, then later a café.

7. Mythological Statues
The large park is dotted with 32 stone statues, created by Christian Beyer between 1753 and 1775. Each one represents a mythological figure.

8. Schönbrunn Park
The French Baroque park was laid out as a large pleasure garden by Nicolaus Jadot and Adrian von Steckhoven during the reign of Maria Theresa. It includes various architectural features.

9. Orangery
Schönbrunn's gardens are home to the second-largest Baroque orangery in the world. It was once used as winter quarters for orange trees, potted plants and various imperial festivities.

10. Schönbrunn Zoo
Founded as early as 1752 as a royal menagerie by Emperor Franz I, this is the world's oldest zoo and is home to some 750 species.

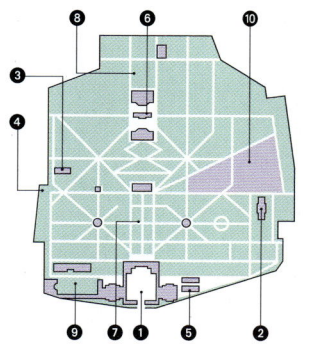

Schönbrunn's Gardens Site Plan

EMPRESS MARIA THERESA AND SCHLOSS SCHÖNBRUNN

Most of the palace as it appears today was created during the reign of Empress Maria Theresa. She ascended the throne in 1740 after her father Charles VI changed the succession to enable females to rule Habsburg countries. The early years of her reign were mainly characterized by foreign political failures as parts of Poland and Italy were lost in wars. But in domestic politics she introduced compulsory education, set up a new administrative structure and improved the social situation for farmers. Maria Theresa was impulsive in her younger years, but after the death of her husband Francis I in 1765 she wore only black mourning gowns and lived a sombre existence. She gave birth to 16 children, 10 of whom survived into adulthood. A noted patron of the visual arts, the empress also loved music, plays and the opera, and presided over Vienna's rise as the musical capital of Europe. In the 1730s, she commissioned a theatre to be built conveniently next to her palace, and on 14 March 1741, the Burgtheater *(p96)*, or Court Theatre, opened its doors for the very first time. Under the rule of Maria Theresa, the Schloss Schönbrunn became the glittering heart of the imperial court. Today, it is considered one of Vienna's most spectacular and popular sights.

**Portrait of Empress
Maria Theresa by
Josef and Mayrhofer
Friedrich Kiss, painted
in 1740, the year of
her ascension to the
royal throne**

TOP 10 OF EVERYTHING

A slice of Sachertorte

PALACES AND HISTORIC BUILDINGS

1 Gartenpalais Liechtenstein

At the end of the 17th century the Liechtenstein family commissioned various architects to build them a summer residence. Designed by Domenico Martinelli and completed in 1692, this Baroque building *(p105)* has been renovated and now houses the private art collection of the Liechtenstein family (mainly 17th-century art).

2 Palais Pallavicini

🚇 M4 🏛 Josefsplatz 5 🔒 To the public 🌐 palais-pallavicini.at

Built at the site of the former Queen's Monastery between 1782 and 1784, this was Vienna's first Neo-Classical building, imitating ancient Greek as well as Roman architectural styles. The formal façade is enlivened by the striking portal with caryatids by Franz Anton von Zauner. The Pallavicini family still live here, and parts of the palace host a congress centre.

3 Augartenpalais

🚇 B5 🏛 Obere Augartenstrasse 1–3 🔒 To the public except Open Day

The Baroque palace in Augarten park is now the home of the Vienna Boys' Choir school and for the most part it is inaccessible to the public.

4 Palais Lobkowitz

🚇 M4 🏛 Lobkowitzplatz 2
🕐 10am–6pm Wed–Mon ♿

Designed by Giovanni Pietro Tencalla, this large Baroque palace was built in 1685 as a stately city mansion for Count Dietrichstein. The Lobkowitz family acquired the palace in 1753. Today, the building is home to the Austrian Theatre Museum, which has exhibitions on costume design, ballet, opera and theatre. It also hosts stage readings and live performances.

5 Palais Schönborn-Batthyány

🚇 L2 🏛 Renngasse 4 🎵 For concerts only, check website 🌐 classical-concerts.at

The palace, designed by Fischer von Erlach between 1699 and 1706, was the home of the Hungarian Batthyány family, who fought for Prince Eugene. The Schönborns acquired it in 1740; today it hosts classical music events.

6 Palais Mollard-Clary

🚇 L2 🏛 Herrengasse 9

This magnificent Baroque palace dating from 1686 owes its name to two aristocratic tenants, Mollard and Clary. This residence was used by Joseph II for his

English-style garden at the Gartenpalais Liechtenstein

famous round-table soirées. It now houses the Austrian Music Collection and the Globe Museum *(p74)*.

7 Palais Daun-Kinsky
🅟 L2 🏛 Freyung 4 🔒 To the public
🌐 palaisevents.at

Baroque architect Johann Lukas von Hildebrandt's most splendid palace (1713–16) was acquired by the Kinsky family in 1784. Today, its lavish rooms host weddings and dinner events.

8 Dorotheum
This grand palace *(p100)*, built in Neo-Baroque style between 1898 and 1901, houses pawnshops and one of Europe's largest auction houses.

9 Palais Trautson
🅟 J4 🏛 Museumstrasse 7
🔒 To the public

Count Trautson had this palace built in 1710–17 in French style; Maria Theresa converted it into guards' headquarters in 1760. Today it is used by the Austrian Justice Ministry.

10 Palais Ferstel
🅟 L2 🏛 Strauchgasse 4
🔒 To the public 🌐 palaisevents.at

This grand building in Historicist style was erected between 1856 and 1860 as a stock exchange for the National Bank. Now part of the palace is the Café Central *(p102)*. The building is sometimes used for gala events.

Sumptuous interior of the Palais Ferstel

TOP 10 EXAMPLES OF ARCHITECTURAL STYLES

Gasometers built in 1896–99

1. Roman Houses
Early houses in Michaelerplatz were built by the Roman garrisons.

2. Medieval House
The Basiliskenhaus *(Schönlaterngasse 7)* is a classic 13th-century dwelling.

3. Renaissance
The portal of the Salvatorkapelle church *(Salvatorgasse 5)* dates back to 1530.

4. Baroque Palaces
Palaces built in richly decorated Baroque style, such as the Belvedere *(p36)*, can be found throughout Vienna.

5. Biedermeier House
The Arabesques and frescoes of this house at Annagasse 11 are typical of the Biedermeier period (1815–1848).

6. Art Nouveau Buildings
The stations of the former city railway were constructed by Otto Wagner *(p127)* in the 1890s.

7. Purist Villa
The Villa Moller *(Starkfriedgasse 19)* by Adolf Loos (1927–8) reflects his principles of the use of space.

8. Council Housing
The massive Karl-Marx-Hof building on Heiligenstädter Strasse was constructed in 1930.

9. Haas-Haus
Hans Hollein's Post-Modernist edifice *(Goldschmiedgasse 3)* is part-mirrored.

10. Gasometer
These brick gas-storage towers *(Guglgasse 6)* were turned into apartments in 2001.

MONUMENTS AND MEMORIALS

1 Johann Strauss Monument
🔲 P5 🏛 Stadtpark, Parkring

Stadtpark (p70) is dotted with monuments of artists and composers, but the gilded 1921 statue of Johann Strauss is allegedly the city's most photographed. The Viennese "Waltz King" is shown playing the violin amid ecstatic dancers and is framed by a marble arch.

2 Schubert's Grave
🏛 Zentralfriedhof, Simmeringer Hauptstrasse 234

Franz Schubert was buried at the Währinger Friedhof in 1828, following his early death aged 31. When the cemetery was closed in 1872, his bones were moved to the Central Cemetery. There he was given an honorary grave among many of his composer friends.

3 Franz Schubert Monument
🔲 Q4 🏛 Stadtpark, Parkring

Franz Schubert is also commemorated with a monument in Stadtpark. It was commissioned by the men's choir Wiener Männergesangsverein, and was created by Carl Kundmann in 1872.

4 Memorial against War and Fascism

The Austrian sculptor Alfred Hrdlicka created a monument (p98) in 1988–91 to commemorate those killed during the National Socialist regime and World War II. Separate elements, made of granite from the area of the Mauthausen concentration camp, are arranged on the square where the Philipphof house was situated. The house was destroyed during an air raid on 12 March 1945 and more than 300 people were buried alive in its debris.

5 Mariensäule Am Hof
🔲 M2 🏛 Am Hof

Am Hof is dominated by a monument to the Virgin Mary (1664–7) that was cast in bronze by Balthasar

Herold. The base shows four angels fighting with four animals, which are symbolic of the four major catastrophes for humankind in the 17th century. The dragon stands for starvation, the lion for war, the fantastical basilisk for the plague, while a snake represents the catastrophe of heresy.

6 Mahler's Grave
📍 Grinzinger Friedhof, An den langen Lüssen 33

Gustav Mahler, director of the Vienna State Opera from 1897 to 1907, was buried at the Grinzinger Friedhof in 1911. The cemetery is in a peaceful location on the outskirts of the city. Mahler's simple white gravestone was designed by his friend, the architect and designer Josef Hoffmann.

7 Maria Theresa Monument
📍 K5 📍 Maria-Theresien-Platz

Between the Kunsthistorisches and Naturhistorisches museums is a statue of Empress Maria Theresa (1717–80). The famed German sculptor Kaspar von Zumbusch created this elaborate monument in 1888, presenting the empress seated on the throne surrounded by ministers and advisors, as well as composers such as Mozart and Haydn.

Edmund von Hellmer's gilded Johann Strauss Monument

8 Klimt's Grave
📍 Hietzinger Friedhof, Maxingstrasse 15

The grave of Secessionist artist Gustav Klimt is found in the Hietzinger Cemetery, located close to Schloss Schönbrunn. Klimt's simple gravestone bears his name in the way he signed his works of art. He died in the year 1918 following a stroke.

9 Schönberg's Grave
📍 Zentralfriedhof, Simmeringer Hauptstrasse 234

The composer Arnold Schönberg (*p67*) has a striking modern cube as his gravestone. It was designed by the Austrian sculptor Fritz Wotruba.

10 Goethe Monument
📍 L5 📍 Opernring/Goethegasse

Next to the Burggarten is a monument to one of the greatest writers in the German language, Johann Wolfgang von Goethe. The statue, seated on a massive base and cast in bronze, was created by Austrian sculptor Edmund von Hellmer in 1900. Also nearby is a memorial statue to another German writer and Goethe's contemporary, Friedrich Schiller.

Goethe Monument at one end of Goethegasse

MUSEUMS

1 Camera and Photography Museum Westlicht

📍 E1 🏛 Westbahnstrasse 40 🕐 2–7pm Tue–Fri (to 9pm Thu), 11am–7pm Sat & Sun 🌐 westlicht.com ✉

Around 800 cameras are on display, including KGB spy cameras disguised as cigarette packets or evening bags.

2 Dom Museum Wien

📍 N3 🏛 Stephansplatz 6 🕐 10am–6pm daily (to 8pm Thu) 🌐 dommuseum.at ✉

Located in the Archbishop's Palace, this museum displays religious art, including 9th-century manuscripts. A huge collection of modern pieces, including works by Chagall, Klimt and contemporary Austrian artists, were added to the museum after it underwent an extensive renovation.

3 Heeresgeschichtliches

📍 Arsenal, Objekt 18 🕐 9am–5pm daily 🌐 hgm.or.at ✉

The Museum of Military History documents the imperial army from the 16th century to 1918.

4 Wien Museum Karlsplatz

📍 F5 🏛 Karlsplatz 🕐 10am–6pm Tue–Sun & public hols 🌐 wienmuseum.at ✉

Set over three storeys, this museum documents the history of Vienna with items spanning 7,000 years.

5 Jüdisches Museum der Stadt Wien

📍 M4 🏛 Palais Eskeles, Dorotheergasse 11 🕐 10am–6pm Sun–Fri 🗓 Jewish hols 🌐 jmw.at ✉

The world's first Jewish museum was founded in Vienna in 1895, but its exhibits were confiscated by National Socialists in 1938. The present museum, housed inside the Palais Eskeles, has a library as well as archives. Nearby, another museum, at Judenplatz, displays excavations of a medieval synagogue.

6 Technisches Museum Wien

📍 G1 🏛 Mariahilfer Strasse 212 🕐 9am–6pm Mon–Fri, 10am–6pm Sat & Sun 🌐 technischesmuseum.at ✉

Opened in 1918, this museum houses more than 80,000 exhibits relating to technology, energy and heavy industry. Highlights include the excellent railway collection, with its extensive array of imperial carriages and engines.

7 Naturhistorisches Museum

Especially enthralling for children and their parents, the fascinating Natural History Museum (p111) is world-class, both for its curious collection, as well as its architecture.

Climbing the piano steps at the the Haus der Musik

Italian Renaissance-style
Naturhistorisches Museum

8 Mozarthaus Vienna

N3 Domgasse 5
10am–6pm daily
mozarthausvienna.at

Mozart occupied a flat on the first floor of the Figarohaus in 1784–7. He composed some of his greatest symphonies here (p66), including The Marriage of Figaro. The museum has exhibitions as well as Mozart's flat.

9 Museum für angewandte Kunst (MAK)

Q3 Stubenring 5 10am–10pm Tue, 10am–6pm Wed–Sun
mak.at

The Austrian Museum of Applied Arts includes world-famous works by the Wiener Werkstätte, an arts and crafts studio from 1870 to 1956. museum, at Judenplatz, displays excavations of a medieval synagogue.

10 Haus der Musik

N5 Seilerstätte 30
10am–10pm daily hdm.at

At the interactive House of Music, visitors are invited to experiment with sounds, to play giant instruments such as an oversized drum, or to "conduct" the Vienna Philharmonic Orchestra. Even the steps on the museum's staircase acts as keys on a piano.

TOP 10 UNUSUAL MUSEUMS

1. Clownmuseum
Ilgplatz 7 circus-clown museum.at
A collection of colourful circus posters, props, costumes and programmes.

2. Fiakermuseum
Veronikagasse 12 fiaker zentrale.at
A museum dedicated to the Viennese horse-drawn carriages known as fiaker.

3. Kriminalmuseum
B5 Grosse Sperlgasse 24
wien.kriminalmuseum.at
Shows the city's most sensational crimes, from the Middle Ages to the present.

4. Schnapsmuseum
H1 Wilhelmstrasse 19–21
Set in an old distillery, this museum is devoted to the Austrian drink, schnapps.

5. Uhrenmuseum
M2 Schulhof 2
Timepieces of all ages and shapes.

6. Josephinum
A collection of anatomical wax models (p106) once used to train surgeons.

7. Pathologisch-Anatomisches Museum
B2 Vienna University Campus, Spitalgasse 2
A former psychiatric ward houses a morbid collection of medical horrors.

8. Third Man Museum
F3 Pressgasse 25
A museum dedicated to the 1949 classic movie The Third Man, filmed in Vienna.

9. Bestattungsmuseum
This undertakers' museum (p74) in Vienna's Zentralfriedhof (Central Cemetery) displays a variety of funereal objects.

10. Kaffeemuseum
H3 Vogelsanggasse 36, A-10 kaffeemuseum.at
This small museum celebrates coffee, the favourite drink of the Viennese.

Egyptian Antiquities Room, Kunsthistorisches Museum

ART GALLERIES

Gustav Klimt and Egon Schiele. The Upper Belvedere displays art from the Middle Ages onwards while the Lower Belvedere houses temporary exhibitions.

3 KunstHaus Wien
📍 Untere Weissgerberstrasse 13 🕐 10am–6pm daily 🌐 kunsthaus wien.com ♿

The only permanent collection of the works of notable Austrian artist Friedensreich Hundertwasser, whose passion for the irregular was largely inspired by Viennese Secessionists, is housed in this privately funded gallery. Located near the famous Hundertwasserhaus (p48), KunstHaus welcomes close to 200,000 visitors a year. The museum's black-and-white façade, uneven floors and roof gardens were designed by the artist himself in 1989.

4 Kunsthistorisches Museum

The impressive imperial art collection is housed in the Kunsthistorisches Museum (p32) and includes one of the world's finest gatherings of works by the Old Masters.

1 Albertina
The Albertina palace (p95) houses a collection of graphic art, architectural drawings and photographs from all periods. The 65,000 drawings and almost one million prints include works by Dürer and Klimt.

2 The Belvedere
This Baroque palace (p36) is home to a wonderful collection of Austrian artworks, including paintings by

Renaissance paintings at the Kunsthistorisches Museum

**The striking entrance of
the Albertina Modern**

5 Albertina Modern

📍 N6 🚇 Karlsplatz 5
🌐 albertina.at

Located in the Künstlerhaus building,
the Albertina Modern houses a vast
collection of modern and contemporary
art. There are over four temporary
exhibitions a year on subjects like
graphic art and photography. Past
exhibitions have included works
by Jackson Pollock, Joan Mitchell,
Ai Weiwei and Valie Export.

6 Akademie der bildenden Künste Art Collections

The Academy of Fine Arts Vienna *(p119)*
possesses collections of Old Masters
(Painting Gallery), as well as prints and
drawings (Graphic Collection). Regular
special exhibitions show selected
works along with contemporary art.

7 Kunsthalle

📍 J5 & F4 🚇 Museums-platz
1 & Treitlstrasse 2 🕐 10am–6pm
Tue–Sun (to 8pm Thu) 🌐 kunsthalle
wien.at 🔗

Specializing in contemporary art, the
Kunsthalle has two venues – one within
the MuseumsQuartier *(p42)* and the
other at Karlsplatz – enabling its curators
to feature several fascinating changing
exhibitions. At the Karlsplatz site, the
exhibits can be seen from the outside,
as the building is made entirely of glass.

8 Museum im Schottenstift

📍 L2 🚇 Freyung 6 🕐 11am–
5pm Tue–Fri, 11am–4:30pm Sat
🚫 Public hols 🌐 schotten.wien 🔗

The Scots' Abbey, founded in 1155 by
Scottish and Irish Benedictine monks,
is a massive complex, containing a
church, a school and a monastery. The
abbey's stunning treasures include tapestries, furniture and many liturgical
objects. Most important of all are the
museum's religious landscape and
portrait paintings from all periods.

9 Kunstforum Bank Austria

📍 L2 🚇 Freyung 8 🕐 10am–
7pm daily (to 9pm Fri) 🌐 kunstforum
wien.at 🔗

Dedicated to the modern classics
and their forerunners, the Kunstforum
organizes several major exhibitions
a year. By presenting shows of world-
famous artists such as Egon Schiele,
Oskar Kokoschka, Paul Cézanne, Pablo
Picasso and Vincent van Gogh, the
gallery has always attracted large
crowds of art lovers.

10 mumok

This gallery *(p43)* is officially
named the Museum Moderner Kunst
Stiftung Ludwig Wien. It contains
one of the largest European collections of modern and contemporary
art, from American Pop Art, Photo
Realism, Fluxus and Nouveau Réalisme
to Viennese Actionism, Arte Povera,
Conceptual and Minimal Art. Tours
in English are held at 4pm on Saturdays
and 2pm on Sundays.

**Modern exterior of mumok
in the MuseumsQuartier**

COMPOSERS

Portrait of Franz Schubert by Gábor Melegh

1 Franz Schubert
The 12th child born in the family home at Nussdorfer Strasse 54, in Vienna, Franz Schubert (1797–1828) composed many symphonies, although it is for his songs that he is best remembered. The tiny two-room flat at No 6 Kettenbrückengasse where he died in 1828 has been now converted into a museum and music studio. It houses a meagre scattering of his personal effects.

2 Joseph Haydn
Along with Beethoven and Mozart, Haydn (1732–1809) is the third important composer of the Vienna Classical period (1750–1830). He moved to Vienna aged eight, to become a choirboy at Stephansdom. In his house at Haydngasse 19 he wrote his greatest works, such as the oratorio *The Creation* (1796–8).

3 Ludwig van Beethoven
When Ludwig van Beethoven (1770–1827) gave his first concert in the Vienna Court Theatre in 1795 he already had a reputation as an excellent pianist. Born in Bonn, he moved to Vienna aged 22 to receive tuition from Joseph Haydn and, briefly, Mozart. In 1805, his opera *Fidelio* premiered at the Theater an der Wien *(p120)*.

4 Anton Bruckner
Born in a village in Upper Austria, Bruckner (1824–96) moved to the capital in 1868, when he became a professor at the city's musical academy. Well respected today, his contemporaries were critical about his music and some of his pieces were never performed during his lifetime.

5 Johannes Brahms
Born in Hamburg in 1833, Brahms became the musical director of the Vienna Singakademie, a choral society, in 1862. For three seasons he directed the Vienna Philharmonic Orchestra, but from 1878 onwards he devoted all of his time to composition. Brahms died in 1897 and is buried at the Zentralfriedhof *(p131)*.

6 Wolfgang Amadeus Mozart
Although born in Salzburg, the life of this world-famous composer (1756–91) is inextricably intertwined with Vienna. Mozart moved to the city in 1781 after falling out with his sponsor, the Archbishop of Salzburg. It was here that he wrote his greatest works and celebrated all his triumphs and misfortunes before he died, aged just 35.

Marble statue of Mozart in the Burggarten

Austro-Bohemian Romantic composer Gustav Mahler

7 Gustav Mahler
Renowned conductor and composer, Mahler (1860–1911) wrote ten symphonies and song cycles in his life. His compositions, including the beautiful *Symphony No. 5*, are some of the most frequently performed works.

8 Johann Strauss II
Vienna's "Waltz King" (1825–99) was the most successful of a dynasty of composers and musicians. He wrote more than 500 dance pieces, among them the *Blue Danube Waltz* (1867), which became Austria's unofficial national anthem. Strauss is buried at the Zentralfriedhof *(p131)*.

9 Arnold Schönberg
Founder of the 12-tone serial technique, Schönberg (1874–1951) became one of the 20th century's most renowned composers. He left Vienna in 1933 in the wake of National Socialism and died in the US.

10 Olga Neuwirth
Born in 1968, Neuwirth is an Austrian composer, visual artist and author. Her operas, such as *Orlando*, based on a novel by Virginia Woolf, are often influenced by literary works. She has also collaborated with her partner, the writer Elfriede Jelinek.

TOP 10
MOZART'S VIENNA

1. Mozartplatz
G4
In the centre of Mozartplatz stands a statue of Mozart, while characters from his opera *The Magic Flute* watch over the square.

2. Tiefer Graben
M2
Mozart stayed at the house at No. 18 on this street during his first concert tour to Vienna in 1762.

3. Palais Collalto
M2   Am Hof 13
A six-year-old Mozart gave his first Vienna concert in this palace in 1762.

4. Griechenbeisl
P2   Fleischmarkt 11
On one of the walls in Vienna's oldest inn you will find Mozart's signature among those of other famous visitors.

5. Stephansdom
Mozart married Constanze Weber on 4 August 1782 in Vienna's impressive cathedral *(p22)*.

6. Café Frauenhuber
N4   Himmelpfortgasse 6
Mozart gave piano concerts in the music room of the café.

7. Mozart's Piano
L4   Neue Burg
Instruments believed to have been played by Mozart are housed in the Sammlung alter Musikinstrumente.

8. Mozart's Grave
Mozart was buried at St Marx Cemetery *(p134)* but the site of his actual grave remains unknown.

9. Mozart Cenotaph
Simmeringer Hauptstrasse
A cenotaph commemorating Mozart was relocated from St Marx Cemetery to the Zentralfriedhof in 1891.

10. Mozarthaus Vienna
Mozart wrote his most famous opera, *The Marriage of Figaro*, here *(p61)*.

UNDERGROUND VIENNA

1 Römermuseum

📍 D4 🏛 Hoher Markt 3
🕐 9am–5pm Tue–Fri, 10am–5pm Sat & Sun ♿

Remains of the ancient Roman camp Vindobona can be seen at this superb underground museum. Excavations show archaeological finds such as pottery and coins.

2 Michaelerkirche Crypt

📍 M3 🏛 Michaelerplatz 4–5
🌐 michaelerkirche.at ♿♿

Well-preserved mummies, some still wearing Baroque frocks and wigs, are preserved in this crypt. From 1631 to 1784, some 4,000 bodies were buried here, including nobles who wanted to rest close to the emperor at Hofburg.

3 Kapuzinergruft

📍 M4 🏛 Tegetthoffstrasse 2
🕐 10am–6pm daily 🌐 kapuzinergruft.com ♿

The crypt present underneath the Kapuzinerkirche (Capuchin Church) was built by Empress Anna in 1618 and served as the burial place of the Habsburgs for over 350 years. Among the 140 elite bodies resting here are 12 emperors and 19 empresses. However, their hearts were removed and buried in silver containers in the crypt of Augustinerkirche and their intestines in copper urns in the catacombs of Stephansdom.

4 Kunst im Prückel

📍 Q3 🏛 Biberstrasse 2 ☎ 01 512 54 00 🕐 8:30am–10pm daily

Hidden away in the basement of the popular vintage coffee house Café Prückel (p102) is this tiny gem of a venue. An eclectic theatre staging intimate drama, cabaret, concerts and literary soirées, it lends a quirky, magical vibe to the neighbourhood.

5 Sewers

📍 M6 🏛 Karlsplatz-Girardipark (U1, U2, U4), opposite the Café Museum 🌐 drittemanntour.at ♿♿

Vienna's sewers came to fame in the 1949 film classic *The Third Man*, when Harry Lime, played by Orson Welles, was chased through the city's underworld by the police. Filmed in postwar Vienna, the movie is still

Exploring Vienna's sewers, made famous in *The Third Man*

remembered today, as several tours follow in the characters' footsteps, taking visitors through various iconic filming locations. Tours are held from May to October; check the website for details.

6 Stephansdom Catacombs

In the 18th century many graveyards across Europe were closed down as plague epidemics spread quickly in the cities. Some cemeteries were relocated beneath city churches, and people's bones were reburied in the crypts. The catacombs *(p23)* under the Gothic Stephansdom were built after Emperor Charles VI shut down the cathedral's graveyard in 1732. They are filled with the bones of some 11,000 people. Today it is hard to imagine that the Stephansplatz was once crammed with gravestones.

7 Virgilkapelle

📍 N3 🚇 Stephansplatz U-Bahn station 🕐 10am–5pm Tue–Sun 🌐 wienmuseum.at ♿

The large Gothic St Virgil's Chapel was only discovered in the 1970s, when the metro line U1 was built – it had been hidden underground for some 200 years. Established in the 1200s, it was used for public burials until a Vienna merchant turned it into his private crypt in the 14th century.

Richly decorated Habsburg tomb in the Kapuzinergruft

8 Cabaret Fledermaus

📍 M3 🚇 Spiegelgasse 2 🌐 fledermaus.at

A long staircase leads down to the Cabaret Fledermaus, named after the bats *(Fledermäuse)* that inhabited Vienna's cellars in the Middle Ages. The venue plays retro music, but there are also themed nights featuring other genres, some with free admission.

9 Augustinerkirche

📍 M4 🚇 Augustinerstrasse 3 (entrance on Josefsplatz) 🕐 8am–6pm daily ♿

St Augustine's Church, built in 1327 in Gothic style, hosted many imperial weddings but the church is most famous for its Herzgruft (hearts' crypt) containing the hearts of Austria's emperors.

10 Wine Cellars

In the Middle Ages, most Vienna houses had as many storeys below ground as they had above. The cellars stored wine, vegetables and other goods. This underground labyrinth was often connected by tunnels. Some cellars continue to exist today as "Keller" restaurants. These include the Rathauskeller at Wipplinger-strasse 8 and the Esterhazykeller at Haarhof 1.

PARKS AND GARDENS

1 Schönbrunn Park
The beautiful grounds of Schloss Schönbrunn (p50) include ponds, fountains and a maze.

2 Stadtpark
P5 Parkring
Vienna's oldest public park, bisected by the River Wien, was designed as an artificial landscape in 1862, with paths winding through grassy areas, past ponds and beautiful shrubs and flowers. Stadtpark is most famous, however, for the statue (p58) of the "King of Waltz", Johann Strauss.

3 Augarten
A5 Obere Augartenstrasse 1
An oasis of style and serenity, Vienna's oldest Baroque park has been open to the public since 1775. Within this park lies the excellent Augarten Porcelain Manufactory and Museum (p74) and a World War II-era anti-aircraft tower.

4 Volksgarten
K3
This garden, located between the Burgtheater and Heldenplatz, is popular with students from the nearby university and office workers on their lunch breaks. Its rose beds bloom spectacularly in spring. The replica of the Temple of Theseus in Athens is used for exhibitions.

5 Burggarten
L5 Josefsplatz 1
Behind the National Library is the pretty Burggarten, landscaped in the formal English style and usually inhabited by sun-worshippers on summer days. Located in the Art Nouveau greenhouse, built in 1901, is a stylish café-bar and restaurant.

Strolling in the lush green Burggarten

Colourful flowerbeds
in the Volksgarten

6 Prater
🚇 Prater, 1020

A former 18th-century imperial hunting ground, the Wurstelprater – known as the Prater – is a large public park today. In 2016 it celebrated 250 years of public access. Leafy walks, fairground rides, food stalls, a Ferris wheel and two racecourses are among its highlights.

7 Alpengarten im Belvedere

This is Europe's oldest alpine garden and is part of the Belvedere (p36). The tiny wild garden, beside the more formal Belvedere gardens, is home to more than 4,000 plants, among them a bonsai collection.

8 Rathauspark
🚇 K2

The park in front of the town hall is busy year round with various festivals, ranging from a Christmas market and ice rink in winter to a summer film and music festival. Many monuments and fountains complement the layout of the park. Another attraction is the large number of centuries-old trees.

9 Tiroler Garten
🚇 H1 🚇 Schloss Schönbrunn

Archduke Johann so admired the Tyrolean landscape and architecture that he ordered that an area within Schönbrunn Park be kept as a natural alpine landscape in the 19th century. Today it has an alpine-style house with a small farm and an orchard.

10 Sigmund Freud Park

This green area (p108) that stretches from Vienna University to the Votivkirche is usually packed with students and picnickers on warm summer days. In the park, a ring of different trees surrounding a granite table and chairs represents the member states of the European Union.

TOP 10
FOUNTAINS

1. Neptunbrunnen
Neptune overlooks cascades at Schönbrunn Palace (p50).

2. Mozartbrunnen
🚇 F4 🚇 Mozartplatz
This delicate Jugendstil fountain depicts scenes from the opera The Magic Flute.

3. Hochstrahlbrunnen
🚇 F5 🚇 Schwarzenbergplatz
The enormous fountain, floodlit on summer nights, was built in 1873.

4. Vermählungsbrunnen
🚇 N2 🚇 Hoher Markt
Josef Emanuel von Erlach built this fountain of marble and bronze in 1732.

5. Andromedabrunnen
🚇 M2 🚇 Old Town Hall, Wipplingerstrasse 8
Sculpted by Georg Raphael Donner in 1741, this fountain, shows Andromeda in the fangs of a sea monster.

6. Pallas Athene Brunnen
🚇 K3 🚇 Dr-Karl-Renner-Ring 3
A statue of the Greek goddess of wisdom towers over the fountain.

7. Danubius Brunnen
🚇 M5 🚇 Albertinaplatz
Part of the Albertina building, the fountain features stories of the Danube.

8. Michaelerplatz Brunnen
🚇 L3
The monumental fountains of the Hofburg, Macht zu Lande and Macht zur See, can be seen at this square.

9. Schutzengelbrunnen
🚇 F4 🚇 Rilkeplatz
Little dragons spout water beneath the angel who gives this fountain its name.

10. Yunus Emre Fountain
🚇 Türkenschanzpark
A gift from the Turkish government, the fountain is decorated in gilt script and beautiful tiles.

OUTDOOR ACTIVITIES

Cycling on Heldenplatz in Central Vienna

1 Cycling

Vienna is one of the world's most bike-friendly cities *(p141)*, with over 1,700 km (1,055 miles) of cycle paths making it easy to explore locations such as the Danube Canal and Danube Island. Bike-friendly infrastructure, including rental services and secure parking, also encourages two-wheeled exploration.

2 Swimming

Vienna boasts some great places to take a dip. The Alte Donau (Old Danube) offers some interesting and scenic spots for refreshing plunges year round, while public pools like the Stadionbad *(wienersportstaetten. at/home/stadionbad)* have family-friendly facilities. For a unique experience, visit the Amalienbad *(01 607 47 47)*, a beautiful Art Deco indoor pool on Reumannplatz.

3 Hiking

Vienna is surrounded by great hiking territory. There are 500 km (310 miles) of trails in the Vienna Woods *(p133)*, a short ride from the city centre, while just an hour from the capital lie the Wiener Hausberge (aka the Vienna Alps) with destinations such as Schneeberg, Raxalpe, Semmering and Gutensteiner Alpen to explore.

4 Climbing

It may not be the first activity that comes to mind when visiting Vienna, but if climbing is your thing, head for the Flakturm *(flakturm-klettern.at)* climbing wall, a 34-m- (112-ft-) tall tower in Esterházy Park. Created from an anti-aircraft tower, it has over 25 routes that are suitable for all abilities.

5 Trampolining

A superb way to entertain the kids, Jumping Danube *(danubejumping.at)* is the world's largest floating trampoline facility, boasting 40 trampolines. It's set just off Danube Island, near the Reichsbrücke, and is fun for all ages. At night, the whole thing is illuminated.

6 Beach Volleyball

Its surprising just how much beach volleyball gets played in land-locked Austria – there are courts across the country and the national team plays on the Volleyball World Pro Beach Tour. If you fancy digging, setting and spiking, head to the courts on the Danube Island or along the Danube River *(beachvolleywien.at)*.

7 Hit the Beach

Though far from the sea, you can still work up a tan on one of Vienna's beaches, artificial strands that line sections of the Danube River. The Danube Island has a family friendly beach, while CopaBeach *(copabeach. wien)* is a resort-like area with sand, sun loungers, bars and other facilities.

8 Running

Whether you fancy a simple jog or are training for a big race, you'll find the route to suit in Vienna. For long easy runs, the 21-km- (13-mile-) long Danube Island embankment is ideal: flat, long and illuminated at night. This is also a great location to get in some speedy intervals. For trail running, head out into the Vienna Woods *(p133)*, where there are plenty of steep climbs and gradual descents with varied surfaces underfoot.

9 Kayaking

Austria has a fair amount of kayaking facilities, but one of the best is the wild-water kayaking canal on a 250-m- (820-ft-) long course between the Neue Donau (New Danube) and the Danube River. It's located at the Vienna Watersports Arena *(viennawatersportsarena.at)* on the southeastern outskirts of the city. The arena has held major kayaking championships but also doubles up as a family waterpark and practice facility.

10 Schönbrunn Maze

The hedge maze in the grounds of Schloss Schönbrunn *(p50)* was once accessible only to Habsburg rulers, but it can now be enjoyed by everyone. The original design dates back to 1720 and still offers an enjoyable challenge for visitors of all ages. Enjoy a bird's-eye view of the maze's intricate patterns from a nearby viewing platform.

Children exploring Schönbrunn Maze

TOP 10 SPORTS TO WATCH

Football players from Austria Wien and Rapid Wien

1. Football
Rapid Wien *(skrapid.at)* and Austria Wien *(fk-austria.at)* play their football in the Austrian Bundesliga.

2. Running
The Vienna City Marathon *(vienna-marathon.com)* takes in many of the city's famous landmarks.

3. Tennis
Catch some of the top players on the ATP Tour at the Erste Bank Open *(erstebank-open.com)* in October.

4. Volleyball
Hotvolleys Wien *(hotvolleys.at)* play their games at the Budocenter Wien.

5. Handball
The city's oldest team, FIVERS *(fivers. at)*, compete in the HLA Meisterliga.

6. Canoeing
Professional canoeing events are often held at the Vienna Watersports Area *(viennawatersportsarena.at)*.

7. Ice Hockey
The aptly named Vienna Capitals *(vienna-capitals.at)* play in the top Austrian ice-hockey league.

8. Basketball
Watch a BC Vienna *(bcvienna.com)* basketball game at the city's Hallmann Dome.

9. American Football
The Vienna Vikings *(viennavikings. com)* have won the Eurobowl an impressive five times.

10. Trotting
The Vienna Trotting Club *(krieau.at)* holds around 20 race days a year.

OFF THE BEATEN TRACK

Augarten Porcelain Manufactory and Museum

1 Globe Museum
🚇 L2 📍 Palais Mollard, Herrengasse 9 🕐 Jun–Sep: 10am–6pm daily; Oct–May: 10am–6pm Tue–Sun (to 9pm Thu) 🌐 onb.ac.at ♿

Among the fascinating collections of worldly exhibits in Vienna is the Globe Museum, which opened in 1956. It is said to be the only museum in the world singularly devoted to globes, with most dating back to before 1850. Marvel at more than 600 terrestrial and celestial globular maps – some as large as an adult.

2 Whoosh Vienna
📍 Im Werd 3/5 🌐 whoosh.wien

This community-focused group celebrates modern Vienna in all its complexity. Visitors can choose from its various offbeat themed walking tours, including ones on secret court-yards, tall towers and the city's most unattractive buildings.

3 Augarten Porcelain Manufactory and Museum
🗺 B6 📍 Obere Augartenstrasse 1 🕐 10am–5pm Mon–Sat 🌐 augarten.com ♿🚻

This fascinating museum charts the history of Vienna porcelain, with exhibits from the imperial manufactory (1718–1866) and its successor Augarten (founded in 1923). Tours of the manufactory are held at 11:30am from Monday to Thursday.

4 Republic of Kugelmugel
📍 Antifaschismusplatz 2, Wiener Prater

No need for a passport to visit this self-proclaimed sovereign micro-nation – an unusual ball-shaped house located in Prater park (p71). The house was built by Austrian artist Edwin Lipburger in 1971 and the Republic status declared in 1976 after Lipburger fell out with the author-ities over building permits. He even printed his own stamps.

5 Bestattungsmuseum
📍 Simmeringer Hauptstrasse 234 🕐 10am–4pm Wed–Fri 🌐 bestattungsmuseum.at

This unusual museum is testament to a proud Viennese funeral tradition. Housed in Europe's second-largest cemetery, it contains a macabre collection of coffins, pall-bearers' attire, skulls and other oddities that celebrate the business of death.

6 Elmayer Dance School
🚇 M3 🏛 Bräunerstrasse 13
🕐 3–8pm daily 📅 School hols
🌐 elmayer.at/en 🔗

Book yourself a lesson at the Elmayer Dance School to master the Viennese waltz. Very soon, you'll be swirling around at 180 beats per minute after 50 minutes of professional tuition here. Call ahead for private lessons.

7 Damage Unlimited
🚇 G3 🏛 Mariahilfer Strasse 23–25 📞 0676 668 18 61 🕐 3–6pm Mon–Fri, noon–6pm Sat

Considered Vienna's answer to Comic Con, Damage Unlimited is where you can play old-fashioned board games or electronic first-person shooters.

8 Johann Strauss Apartment
🚇 C6 🏛 Praterstrasse 54 🕐 10am–1pm, 2–6pm Tue–Sun & public hols 🌐 wienmuseum.at

Located in the Leopoldstadt, this apartment was the home of Austrian composer Johann Strauss II. This was where he composed, among other works, the famous *Blue Danube Waltz*, Austria's unofficial national anthem. Exhibits here include manuscripts, furniture and a valuable Amati violin.

Relaxing along the bank of the Donaukanal

9 Summer Beaches
Few visitors know that Vienna has a fine collection of beaches. For some downtime in summer on the city's artificial sandbanks, simply bring a picnic, sunscreen and a swimsuit to one of the half a dozen different venues along the Donaukanal.

10 Stock im Eisen
🚇 N3

In the Middles Ages, trees were studded with nails for good luck; the nails were valuable, and the tree served as an offering to God. A 600-year-old trunk of such a tree is displayed behind protective glass on Stephansplatz, on the corner of Graben and Kärntner Strasse, situated near the striking Palais Equitable mansion.

Elegant interior of the Johann Strauss Apartment

FAMILY ATTRACTIONS

1 Marionettentheater Schönbrunn

📍 G1 🏛 Hofratstrakt, Schloss Schönbrunn 🌐 marionetten theater.at ↗

The puppet theatre in the little court theatre at Schönbrunn stages wonderful shows that delight children and adults alike. A version of Mozart's *The Magic Flute* is the undisputed highlight of the programme, with a feather-clad Tamino and a fantastic vicious snake.

2 Riesenrad

🏛 Prater 90 🕐 May–Aug: 9am–midnight daily; Sep–Apr: hours vary, check website 🌐 wienerriesenrad.com ↗

Over 100 years old, Vienna's giant Ferris wheel at the Prater *(p71)* offers fantastic views over the city's rooftops. Be sure to visit the small museum in the entrance area, where the history of the wheel and the city are told in some of the Riesenrad's old red cabins.

Iconic Riesenrad Ferris wheel at Prater

3 Haus des Meeres

📍 F2 🏛 Esterhazypark 🕐 9am–8pm daily (to 9pm Thu) 🌐 haus-des-meeres.at ↗

Fish and reptiles from all across the world have found a home in a former anti-aircraft tower in Esterhazypark. You can "journey" from the chilly North Sea to the Australian Great Barrier Reef, taking in the natural landscape en route. Very popular with kids are the sharks' and piranhas' feeding time in the "Amazon pool".

4 Hütteldorfer Bad

🏛 Linzer Strasse 376 🕐 8am–9pm daily 🌐 wien.gv.at/ freizeit/hallenbaeder

This municipal swimming pool offers many attractions for children, such as adventure streams, slides and water cannons. A large outdoor play area is open during summer months.

5 Schloss Schönbrunn

Young visitors are given a glimpse of imperial life at Schloss Schönbrunn *(p50)* from a child's perspective at the palace's Children's Museum *(kaiser kinder.at)*. In the Court Bakery, they can watch confectioners make cakes and pastries, which can be sampled fresh from the oven.

**Marionettentheater
Schönbrunn puppet show**

6 Schönbrunn Zoo
Considered the oldest zoo *(p52)* in the world, this has all the usual favourites, including elephants, reptiles and butterflies. Most are housed in Baroque-style compounds.

7 Schönbrunn Park
This beautiful park *(p52)* is home to two special attractions – the maze and the labyrinth. The maze is based on the original 18th-century designs and its tracks through the hedges lead to a wonderful viewing platform in the middle that overlooks the area. The labyrinth is a games zone featuring a giant kaleidoscope, a climbing pole and fun riddles.

8 Technisches Museum Wien
A special adventure area at Vienna's Museum of Technology *(p60)* is geared towards children aged two to eight years old (although older kids enjoy it too) and allows young visitors to actively engage with the technical sciences behind road, maritime and air transport, as well as space exploration. The museum also features a full calendar of events and free-of-charge workshops in the museum's kindergarten. The "crazy laboratory" workshops are highly sought-after.

9 ZOOM
Designed exclusively for children, ZOOM *(p43)* is a place of playful enquiry, learning and discovery. Hands-on exhibitions for toddlers, kitchens for cooking experiments and the chance to "zoom" in on new situations and learn about the world are just some of the highlights at this interactive museum. Booking ahead is recommended.

10 Schmetterlinghaus
📍 L5 🚇 Burggarten, Burgring 🕐 10am–3:45pm daily (Apr–Oct: to 5:45pm) 🌐 schmetterlinghaus.at 📷

This large Art Nouveau greenhouse contains more than 150 species of tropical butterflies and moths, living in microclimatic habitats that replicate their natural environment.

Common tree nymph butterfly at the Schmetterlinghaus

LOCAL DISHES

One of the many Frankfurter stands found throughout Vienna

1 Frankfurters
The takeaway sausage stall, or *würstelstand*, is found all over Vienna. Slim, pale sausages were introduced to Vienna in 1798 by the butcher Johann Georg Lahner, who named them after the city of Frankfurt, where they originated. They are served with mustard and a *semmel* (bread roll).

2 Wiener Schnitzel
The roots of the *Wiener schnitzel* lie in ancient Byzantium, where meat was purportedly eaten after being sprinkled with gold. Over the course of time the precious metal was replaced by a coat of golden breadcrumbs. Count Radetzky, who fought several wars for the Austrian Empire in the 19th century, is said to have brought the dish to imperial Vienna from Milan. The outcome is tasty veal or pork covered in breadcrumbs and fried until golden. The classic side dish is potato salad.

3 Leberknödelsuppe
Austrians are fond of their soups and a traditional three-course Sunday lunch will often start off with a bowl of clear beef broth. This particular variety, served with little liver dumplings, is undoubtedly the best among Austrian soups.

4 Zwiebelrostbraten
Slices of roast beef are topped with fried onion rings and served with mashed or roasted potatoes. A variation is *vanillerostbraten*, in which the meat is seasoned with garlic.

5 Frittatensuppe
Most soups are made of clear beef stock and are served with a range of garnishes to create some variety. Adding *frittaten* – pancakes seasoned with a sprinkle of fresh herbs, cut into thin strips and served in bouillon – is a popular option.

6 Knödel
Vienna's many dumpling types, both sweet and savoury, include plain *knödel* with vegetables and meat, *germknödel* (dumpling with sour prune jam), *zwetschgenknödel* (plum dumpling), *topfenknödel* (curd cheese dumpling) and *griessnockerl* (semolina dumpling).

Traditional dessert of *zwetschgenknödel*

***Tafelspitz*, Franz Joseph's favourite dish**

7 Tafelspitz

Meat is essential to Viennese cuisine, and beef has played a significant role throughout the centuries. The favourite among the many variations is *tafelspitz* – boiled rump, usually served with *rösti* (fried grated potatoes) or boiled potatoes and apple and horseradish sauce. Emperor Franz Joseph allegedly ate it every single day.

8 Gefüllte Paprika

Stuffed peppers are a remnant of the Austro-Hungarian monarchy, when Vienna hosted people from all over Europe. Originally from the Balkans, the dish soon became popular across the city. Green peppers are stuffed with minced meat and rice, and are usually served with a delicious tomato sauce.

9 Schweinsbraten mit Semmelknödel

Roast pork is another standard of Viennese cuisine. It is variously seasoned with flavours ranging from garlic to fresh herbs and caraway, and the meat is generally served with dumplings, salad and gravy.

10 Gulasch

This dish is a successful marriage of Austrian and Hungarian cuisines. The original Hungarian soup-like dish arrived in Viennese kitchens and evolved into goulash – a spicy beef stew, seasoned with paprika and served with dumplings or bread rolls. It can also come with potatoes or a fried egg and gherkins.

TOP 10 VIENNESE CAKES

1. Schwarzwälderkirschtorte
Black Forest Gateau is a rich chocolate cake with layers of sponge, cream and sour cherries.

2. Gugelhupf
With almonds, cocoa or chocolate icing, this cake is baked in a fluted ring mould and is named for its shape.

3. Cremeschnitte
This consists of two layers of crispy puff pastry filled with a thick layer of vanilla-flavoured whipped cream.

4. Dobostorte
This cake features eight layers of light sponge joined together with chocolate cream and glazed with caramel.

5. Linzertorte
Named after the Austrian city of Linz, this almond pastry filled with jam has been popular for nearly 300 years.

6. Malakofftorte
Cream and sponge biscuits drenched in rum are set together and then smothered in buttercream icing.

7. Esterhazytorte
This cake is made with almond sponge layers filled with cream and covered with marbled icing.

8. Rehrücken
The name of this chocolate cake is inspired from its baking mould, which is shaped like the saddle of a deer. It is usually filled with apricot jam.

9. Sachertorte
Confectioner Franz Sacher allegedly invented this rich cake, covered with apricot jam and chocolate.

10. Apfelstrudel
Strudel is an Austrian staple. Very thin dough is sprinkled with apples, cinnamon, raisins and icing sugar.

Slice of apfelstrudel

COFFEE HOUSES

**Posters lining the wall
at Café Hawelka**

Peter Altenberg gathered a literary circle and even had his mail delivered here. Leon Trotsky was also one of the regulars during his Vienna exile prior to World War I. Today the Central serves almost 1,000 cups of coffee a day in its charming and elegant setting.

1 Café Hawelka
Bustling Hawelka *(p102)*, opened in the 1930s, has old-world charm. The owners often took paintings from artists in exchange for food. As a result the walls are covered with works by Ernst Fuchs, among others.

2 Café Museum
Designed by the minimalist architect Adolf Loos in 1899, this café *(p122)* reflects his anti-ornamental aesthetic, and was once the haunt of artists including Klimt and Schiele. Remodelled in the 1930s, it has since been returned to its original design.

3 Café Central
One of the city's best-known cafés, the Central *(p102)* was the meeting place for Vienna's intellectuals at the turn of the 19th century – the poet

4 Café Europa
This café *(p122)* has the amenities of a traditional coffee house, but with modern furnishings and a cheerful informality. It is known for being open until 5am, providing both pastries and cooked meals around the clock. There's also an American-style cocktail bar.

5 Café Landtmann
Franz Landtmann opened his café *(p102)* in 1873. Sigmund Freud used to have his morning coffee here, as did the artistic director of the Burgtheater, Max Reinhardt. Landtmann bustles with activity day and night – it has a large shaded terrace, and the four interior rooms are elegantly decorated with velvet upholstery, starched linen tablecloths, crystal light fixtures and large mirrors with inlaid wood.

6 Café Sperl
Built in grand style in 1880, Sperl *(p122)* has long been a haunt of artists and musicians from the

Entrance to the traditional Viennese Café Sperl

nearby Theater an der Wien. It hosts live piano music every Sunday afternoon from September to June.

7 Café Demel
This café (p102), part of which resembles a Rococo-period salon, is one of Vienna's most refined retreats for cake lovers. Opened in 1786, it had become a hot spot for the Viennese upper classes by the mid-19th century, even providing the beloved Empress Sisi with her favourite sweet violet sorbet.

8 Café Diglas
Established in 1923, the Diglas (p102) has marble tables, wooden chairs and little window booths fitted with red velvet sofas. Ordering a piece of cake – served with a small mountain of whipped cream – is recommended.

9 Café Prückel
Famous for its 1950s-style interior, this classy café (p102) offers excellent Viennese cuisine, and hosts live classical music and plays in its atmospheric basement.

10 Café Bräunerhof
This place (p102) has a traditional living-room atmosphere, cosy but worn, thanks to a stream of customers dating back to the 1900s. It has always been a literary café – the writers Alfred Polgar and Hugo von Hofmannsthal were regulars.

Patrons enjoying a meal at Café Central

TOP 10
TYPES OF COFFEE

1. Eiskaffee
For this drink, cold coffee is served with vanilla ice cream and whipped cream in a tall glass.

2. Grosser Brauner
A large cup of black coffee, steamed like an espresso, and served with a tiny jug of cream on the side.

3. Kleiner Brauner
This is the smaller version of the *Grosser Brauner* and is also served with cream.

4. Grosser Schwarzer
The drink for real coffee addicts – a large, strong cup of black coffee, like a double espresso.

5. Kleiner Schwarzer
As the smaller version of the *Grosser Schwarzer*, this is simply a small cup of black coffee, similar to an espresso.

6. Verlängerter
This is the "lengthened" variety of a *Brauner*, a coffee weakened slightly with hot water and served with milk instead of cream.

7. Kaisermelange
Not to everyone's taste, a *Kaisermelange* is a strong black coffee mixed with egg yolk, honey and Cognac.

8. Einspänner
In this famous drink, strong black coffee is served in a glass with a crown of whipped cream on top.

9. Fiaker
A large cup of coffee is refined with rum and whipped cream. It is named after the city's horse-drawn carriages.

10. Melange
This is a blend of strong coffee and hot milk, served with foamed milk or whipped cream on the top.

***Melange* with whipped cream**

HEURIGEN

1 Sirbu

🏠 Kahlenberger Strasse 210
🕐 Sun & Nov–Mar 🌐 sirbu.at · €

Perched on Kahlenberg mountain (*p132*), this *heuriger* (wine tavern) is set amid luscious vineyards, and is lovely at night. The usual *heurigen* dishes and home-grown wines are served here.

2 Hengl-Haselbrunner

🏠 Iglaseegasse 10 🌐 hengl-haselbrunner.at · €€

Grinzing (*p133*) was once a small community of wine-growers, but now it has one of the highest densities of *heurigen* in Vienna. Slightly off the beaten track, Hengl-Haselbrunner offers excellent red and white wines, plus a buffet of regional specialities.

3 Wieninger

🏠 Stammersdorfer Strasse 31
🕐 Nov–mid-Apr 🌐 heuriger-wieninger.at · €€

This family business serves excellent wines that perfectly complement great food. Largely frequented by locals, Wieninger is less expensive than *heurigen* located in the more famous communities of Grinzing and Nussdorf.

4 Kierlinger

🏠 Kahlenberger Strasse 20
🌐 kierlinger.at · €

The white wines of this traditional tavern are counted among Vienna's best – be sure to sample a glass of their Chardonnay or Weissburgunder. Kierlinger is also known for its tasty Liptauer spread, made of cheese with paprika, onions, gherkins and spices.

The *heuriger* has a large garden, and cultural events take place in the evening all year round.

5 Mayer am Pfarrplatz

🏠 Pfarrplatz 2 🌐 pfarrplatz.at · €€

The historic building now occupied by Mayer am Pfarrplatz was once the home of Ludwig van Beethoven (*p66*). He spent the summer of 1817 here when he hoped to find relief for his worsening deafness. Today, you can soak up the atmosphere and dine on excellent food and home-produced wines. It's an acclaimed winery and has won many national and international prizes. Traditional Viennese live music is played every Friday at 7pm.

6 Fuhrgassl-Huber

🏠 Neustift am Walde 68
🌐 fuhrgassl-huber.at · €€

With seating for 800 people, this busy *heuriger*, located on the edge of the Vienna Woods, is one of the city's largest wine taverns. Glasses of the most recent vintage can be accompanied with food from the buffet, which serves everything from smoked ham to delicious *Wiener schnitzel (p78)*.

7 Zahel

🏠 Maurer Hauptplatz 9
🕐 Sun 🌐 zahel.at · €

The flavourful and aromatic reds and whites from Zahel, a charming winery, should not be missed. This *heuriger's* buffet has a varying selection of à la carte dishes.

Patrons enjoying the
wine and the view at Sirbu

8 Weingut Heuriger Muth
Probusgasse 10 · muth-heuriger.at · €€

This *heuriger* is one of Vienna's oldest wine taverns. It has a large and shady outdoor seating area that is perfect for relaxing in the summer, and often hosts live music performances and events.

9 Christ
Amtsstrasse 14
weingut-christ.at · €

The Christ family has been producing wine for 400 years, winning many awards. Traditional and cosy with a peaceful garden, this *heuriger* serves a wide range of excellent wines and seasonal traditional food, such as asparagus, mushroom or game.

10 Zimmermann
Mitterwurzergasse 20
Mon & Nov–mid-Mar · weinhof-zimmermann.at · €

In rural isolation on the edge of the Vienna Woods, Zimmermann has a zoo with all sorts of small animals, and there is a great friendly, family atmosphere. Enjoy a glass of the new vintages with dishes from the buffet and, in summer, sit out amid the pretty Neustift vineyards. In autumn, there's also a stone fireplace fuelled with birchwood.

Outdoor seating in the
garden at Zimmermann

TOP 10 DRINKS

Bottles of schnapps

1. Schnapps
A distilled eau de vie made from fruits such as apricots or juniper berries.

2. Red Wines
Austria also produces excellent red wines, including Zweigelt, Blauer Portugieser and Blaufränkisch.

3. Gespritzter
Sparkling water mixed with table wine is an all-time favourite in Austria, particularly in summer.

4. Sparkling Wines
The Austrian sparkling wine Sekt is an increasingly popular drink.

5. Beers
Breweries in Vienna produce good, malty beers. Restaurants and bars usually offer a *Seidl* (0.33 litre/0.7 pt) or a *Krügel* (0.5 litre/1pt).

6. Soft Drinks
Apple juice and grape juice mixed (*gespritzt*) with sparkling water is popular, as is *Almdudler*, a lemonade.

7. Sturm
For a few short weeks in autumn, fermenting grape juice is available. Although it tastes sweet, it is alcoholic and quite powerful.

8. Mulled Wines
Around Christmas, hot spicy wine and punch are very popular.

9. Coffee
The city's coffee-house culture was awarded UNESCO status in 2011.

10. White Wines
Austria's superb sweet dessert wines are among the world's best. The main varieties are Grüner Veltliner and Weissburgunder.

For price categories, see p103

LOCAL BUYS

Beautiful gilded glass pitcher by Lobmeyr

1 Glass and Crystal

Vienna has a long tradition of glass and crystal production that largely dates back to the 18th century. The flagship store of Lobmeyr *(Kärntner Strasse 26)*, a company famous for creating intricate crystal chandeliers and glassware, is an Aladdin's cave of treasures.

2 Porcelain

Established in 1718, the Wiener Porzellanmanufaktur *(augarten.com)* is the top name when it comes to fine ceramics. It is famous for its high-quality, hand-painted porcelain, and produces exquisite pieces such as dinnerware, figurines and decorative items, often adorned with intricate patterns and gilded designs. The main shop for their wares is in the Augarten at Obere Augartenstrasse 1.

3 Chocolate, Pralines and Other Sweets

Austria is well-known for producing some iconic sweet treats. Manner *(manner.com)* is famous for its hazelnut wafers, while Heindel *(heindl.co.at)* is the creator of Mozartkugeln, or Mozart Balls, a traditional treat consisting of balls of marzipan, nougat and pistachio slathered in dark chocolate. The other big name to look out for is Demel *(demel.com)*, a historic confectionery maker that is best known for its luxurious pralines, including rich ganache-filled varieties that are crafted with some of the finest ingredients.

4 Sachertorte

Sachertorte is a classic Austrian chocolate cake, first created in 1832 by Franz Sacher for Prince Metternich. It consists of luxuriously rich chocolate sponge layers glued together with apricot jam, the whole thing then smothered in a smooth, chocolate glaze. Traditionally, it's served with a dollop of whipped cream. The best place to buy a slice, or the whole thing, is the Café Sacher *(p146)*, where it was first crafted almost two centuries ago.

5 Antiques

Vienna has countless antiques shops selling high-end, often rare and generally very pricey pieces. Better bargains are to be had in the city's interesting flea markets *(p85)*, where a rummage can often produce retro results.

6 Fashion

Vienna isn't usually synonymous with fashion, but there are plenty of independent shops where you can pick up unique pieces. Arnold's *(arnolds vienna.com)* is a men's outfitters offering that typically smart-casual Vienna look, the wonderfully named Disaster Clothing *(shop-disaster clothing.at)* offers funky pieces by Austrian designers, while NFive *(nfive.at)* stocks obscure labels.

Bags of Mozartkugeln, or Mozart Balls

**Swarovski's flagship store
on Kärntner Strasse**

7 Jewellery
The biggest name in Austrian jewellery is Swarovski (*kristallwelten. swarovski.com*), and the company's flagship store on Kärntner Strasse is a wonderful place to visit, even if you're not in the market for a made-in-Tyrol necklace or pair of earrings.

8 Designer Houseware
Though most items won't fit in your hand luggage, Vienna has a number of houseware boutiques that are fun to peruse, including Inner Space (*Neubaugasse 55*) and Amba (*Langegasse 74*).

9 Viennese Wines
Vienna is the only city in the world to have a notable wine industry within its limits. Austria's wines aren't usually exported even within Europe, making local wines an interesting souvenir. You can pick up a bottle or two from *Heurigen (p82)*, out in the Vienna Woods, from specialist shops or from high-end grocery stores and markets.

10 Apricot products
Austrian apricot products are renowned for their quality, with the Wachau, Weinviertel, Burgenland and Styria providing ideal conditions for cultivation. Apricot-based foods such as jams, preserves and spreads make for unusual souvenirs. Apricot liqueur (*Marillenschnaps*) and apricot strudel are also popular and unique.

TOP 10
MARKETS

1. Naschmarkt
Vienna's top market (*p120*) is stacked high with exotic goodies and eateries.

2. Karmelitermarkt
A4 Karmelitermarkt 21
This large market just to the north of the Innere Stadt has some great finds.

3. Rochusmarkt
R4 Landstrasser Hauptstrasse 3
This small but very popular farmers' market is in the Landstrasse District.

4. Kutschkermarkt
B1 Kutschkergasse
One of Vienna's two remaining street markets, Kutschkermarkt is known for its gourmet produce and flowers.

5. Hannovermarkt
Hannovermarkt 1
Around since 1850, this market is best visited on Fridays and Saturdays.

6. Brunnenmarkt
Brunnengasse 16
With 170 stalls between Thaliastrasse and Ottakringer Strasse, this is Vienna's biggest street market.

7. Meiselmarkt
Hütteldorferstrasse 81b
This covered market in the western suburbs is worth the journey for its quality produce.

8. Meidlinger Markt
Meidling
This old Viennese market has lots of eateries and a farmers' market feel.

9. Naschmarkt Flea Market
Visit the Naschmarkt (*p120*) on Saturday for its huge flea market.

10. Vienna Christmas Markets
The capital's atmospheric Advent markets (*p91*) are held at various locations around the city centre.

A stall in the Naschmarkt

NIGHTS OUT

1 Theatre Nights
For a sophisticated night out in Vienna, a trip to the theatre is difficult to beat. The city offers a huge range of performances, and in the Burgtheater (p96), it has one of Europe's oldest and most prestigious theatres – dating back to 1741, this was once the top stage in the empire. The building is known for its magnificent Baroque architecture and for the quality of the classical and contemporary performances it hosts on a nightly basis. You won't be the only one trying to catch a performance here, so make sure you book your tickets well in advance.

2 Catch some Classical Music
Wolfgang Amadeus Mozart, Johann Strauss and Gustav Mahler are some of the main reasons music fans visit Vienna, and a classical music concert in the erstwhile home of such giants of the genre is an unmissable experience. The Musikverein (p125) is the best place to go, the programme a guarantee of quality. The concert hall has superb acoustics and is home to the Vienna Philharmonic; it also hosts the iconic New Year's Concert.

3 Go to the Opera
The opera has always been a firm favourite among local audiences, who head to the Volksoper Wien (volksoper.at) and Staatsoper (p44) for their operatic fix. Mozart is the name everyone associates with the world of Viennese opera and a performance of *Idomeneo*, *Don Giovanni* or *The Marriage of Figaro* is a quintessential experience.

4 Pop out for a Beer
Vienna's pub scene is that classic Central European mix of tradition and modernity, offering something for everyone. Typical Viennese beer halls serve local brews like Ottakringer, while craft-beer bars experiment with brews of varying styles. Vienna's cosy pubs, often decorated in traditional timber style, provide an intimate atmosphere for nights out. Head to the bustling Bermuda Triangle (p101) for diverse bars and kicking nightlife.

5 Late Openings
You don't necessarily need to limit your sightseeing to daylight hours in Vienna, as the city has numerous attractions that stay open long after the sun has set. The Prater (p71) fair

The Barqoue Burgtheater, one of Europe's oldest theatres

comes alive after dark, when the place is atmospherically illuminated, while the terrace at Donauturm (p134) is open until 10:30pm, giving visitors views of Vienna prettily lit up below.

6 Hit the Clubs

Vienna's club scene is a surprisingly dynamic blend of sophistication and energy, with everything from sleek underground techno venues to thumping hip-hop and pop clubs. Many clubs also blend in art and culture, creating a unique after-dark experience. Popular spots like Pratersauna (pratersauna.tv) and Grelle Forelle (grelleforelle.com) are renowned for their international DJ sets and pulsating atmospheres.

7 Amazing Live Music

Vienna's music scene isn't just classical. Jazzland (p101) and Porgy & Bess (porgy.at) are both big hitters in Austrian jazz circles. For a mixed bag of rock, indie, cabaret and pop, both Austrian and international, Szene Wien (szene.wien) is the place to seek out. For big-name concerts by stars current and former, the Stadthalle (stadthalle.com) is the premium venue, playing host to artists and bands such as James Blunt, Simply Red and Billie Eilish.

A performance in the convivial surroundings of Jazzland

The fairground attractions at Prater, atmospherically lit up at night

8 Soak up the LGBTQ+ scene

Celebrated for its progressive attitudes and diverse communities, Vienna offers one of Central Europe's more vibrant LGBTQ+ scenes. Thanks in part to the city's safe and welcoming environment, there are numerous gay-friendly bars, clubs and cafés here, particularly in the Mariahilf and Neubau districts. Vienna Pride and Rainbow Parade (viennapride.at) are annual highlights, attracting thousands of revellers each year.

9 Danube Dinner Cruise

Experience a magical evening on the Danube by taking a dinner cruise with DDSG Blue Danube (ddsg-blue-danube.at). Gliding along Europe's most famous river, illuminated sights passing by, you can enjoy exquisite Austrian cuisine paired with local wines. Live music accompanies the journey, making it the perfect way to spend a romantic evening in Vienna.

10 Night at the Museum

Thursday night is late-opening night across Vienna, and that goes for the institutions that populate the MuseumsQuartier (p42), too. Most of the museums and cultural attractions here stay open until 9pm, great if you haven't managed to see everything you wanted to during the day.

VIENNA FOR FREE

1 Magical Music
Every summer in June, free open-air concerts include the Vienna Philharmonic Orchestra hosting the Sommernachtskonzert *(wienerphilhar moniker.at)* at the Schloss Schönbrunn gardens and three days of live music at Europe's biggest party at Donauinsel *(donauinselfest.at)*. Meanwhile, the Fest der Freude *(festderfreude.at)* sees the Wiener Symphoniker orchestra perform on Heldenplatz.

2 Danube Dipping
The beach at the tip of the summer party island of Donauinsel in the middle of the Danube river is a designated FKK zone for clothing-optional sunbathing. FKK stands for *freikörperkultur*, meaning "culture of free bodies". Stripping off in this verdant waterfront setting costs nothing and you can also drink at the bars here *au naturel*.

3 Schloss Schönbrunn Gardens
Although entry to Vienna's grandest palace is pricey, visitors can stroll the delightful gardens for free. Schloss Schönbrunn *(p50)* is a horticultural wonder, with sumptuous planting and pretty fountains.

4 Tours of the Rathaus
Free state-room tours of Vienna's Rathaus *(p113)* reveal some of the city's lesser-known political secrets and are rich in controversy, power struggles and mayoral intrigue.

5 Walking Tour
Take advantage of the city's only free walking tour, departing four days a week from the Wombat's hostel *(wombats-hostels.com)* in Naschmarkt. It's a great way to gain fascinating insights into the city and for solo travellers to make new friends.

6 The Hofburg
While many of the dazzling imperial residences of the Hofburg palace *(p26)* charge for entry, the stunning maze of stone passages, Michaelerkirche and Augustinerkirche can be visited for free.

7 Sankt-Marxer-Friedhof
Take a leisurely stroll around the famous St Marx Cemetery *(p134)*. Among the medieval tombs, burial chambers and carved crosses, you'll spot a gravestone that honours Wolfgang Amadeus Mozart (ironically, given the beloved composer's stature

Fairground attractions at Prater park

today, his body is thought to be buried elsewhere in a pauper's grave).

8 Museum Entry
The Kunsthistorisches Museum (*p32*), the Belvedere palaces (*p36*), the Naturhistorisches Museum (*p111*) and several others in Vienna offer free entry to under 19s. Most museums are free on National Day (26 October).

9 Cinematic Splendour
Vienna runs atmospheric open-air cinema screenings of opera, ballet and classical music from July to August at an open-air cinema in the Rathausplatz, with pop-up food stalls supplying tasty treats. There's also a giant screen on Herbert-von-Karajan Platz (*wien.info*), which shows Staatsoper (*p44*) opera and ballet concerts all summer.

10 Prater
It doesn't cost a penny to wander around the Prater (*p71*). This large public park has pleasant tree-lined avenues, verdant meadows and a maze of cycling paths waiting to be explored. The 200 or so attractions are each paid for separately, but you can soak up the magic, music and mayhem of the fairground atmosphere for free.

Open-air concert in the gardens at Schloss Schönbrunn

TOP 10
BUDGET TIPS

1. Make use of the free hour's bike hire from WienMobil Bike, Vienna's excellent public rental scheme (*p141*). Pick up a bike from one of the docking stations and return it to another station within an hour.

2. For a cheaper alternative to an open-top bus ride take the tram (*p140*): a scenic option at a fraction of the price.

3. Pick up a money-saving Vienna City Card (*p145*) for free entry to over 60 top attractions, museums and monuments plus various discounts on travel.

4. Maximize cheap travel by avoiding peak travel times and buying a multiday travel pass (*p139*) for 24, 48 or 72 hours.

5. To take a self-guided walking tour, download a free map from City Walks (*city-walks.info/Vienna*). A stroll along the Danube Canal, Vienna's open-air gallery, lets you admire the quirky graffiti adorning its banks.

6. Make your way to Neubau (*p112*) for the city's best cheap eats. Some places charge only what you can afford to pay.

7. Don't waste your money on bottled water as Vienna's high-quality drinking water – free from fountains across the city – comes straight from sparkling mountain springs.

8. No need to rack up hefty mobile bills while you're exploring Vienna as free Wi-Fi hotspots are available in almost all central public places.

9. Last-minute cut-priced theatre and music tickets are available from venues on the day (*viennaconcerts.com*).

10. Visit the Saturday flea market (*flohmarkt*) in the Naschmarkt (*p120*) for unique shoestring bargains.

FESTIVALS

Contemporary dance performance at ImPulsTanz

1 Easter Markets
Mar/Apr

Austria's Easter tradition is to decorate branches of pussy willow with painted eggshells hung on string. Easter Egg Markets are also held on squares and in front of churches.

2 Wiener Festwochen
May/Jun

This annual festival held at venues including the MuseumsQuartier (*p42*), the Ronacher and Theater an der Wien (*p120*) includes theatre and dance productions.

3 Jazzfest
Mid-Jun–early Jul

Traditional homes of classical music such as the State Opera and the Konzerthaus (*konzerthaus.at*) turn into jazz venues during the annual Jazzfest, where you can see world-famous jazz musicians perform all over the city.

4 Oper Klosterneuburg
Jul

This festival stages glamorous performances of opera classics in the courtyard of Klosterneuburg abbey (*p134*), the palatial religious foundation that dominates the town of the same name just north of Vienna. There are also fascinating behind-the-scenes workshops for children.

5 MusikFilmFestival
Jul–Aug

Every year the square in front of Vienna's Town Hall (*p113*) turns into a bustling hub for music lovers. Every evening crowds flock to watch pop concerts, musicals, ballet, opera and operetta performances broadcast on a huge screen. Just as popular are the many food stalls where Mexican, Japanese, Greek as well as Austrian specialities can all be found.

6 ImPulsTanz
Jul–Aug

Vienna turns into the capital of dance when the international dance festival takes place at venues such as the Burg and Akademietheater.

7 Viennale
Oct

Vienna's international film festival, the Viennale, features pre-release and independent films from around

Christmas market with the Karlskirche in the backdrop

Guests at the city's most glamorous ball in Staatsoper

the world. Screenings take place at the Gartenbau, Urania and Metro cinemas, among other venues.

8 Wien Modern
Late Oct–Nov
Wien Modern is one of few genuinely successful festivals for post-1945 and contemporary "classical" music in Europe.

9 Christmas Markets
Nov–Dec
In the weeks leading up to Christmas you'll find numerous festive markets across Vienna's squares and pedestrianized zones. The stalls sell small gifts and Christmas decorations, as well as punch and hot spiced wine.

10 Ball Season
Dec–Feb
Viennese life revolves around the waltz, at least between Christmas and Lent, when the calendar is full with evenings of dancing. Balls in the Hofburg palace are the most splendid, but there are dances in many of Vienna's hotels and, once a year, in the Staatsoper (p44).

TOP 10
RELIGIOUS FESTIVALS

1. Epiphany
6 Jan
Children dress as the Three Wise Men and bring news of Christ's birth. Special services are held in churches across the city to celebrate the event.

2. Easter
Mar/Apr
The resurrection of Christ is celebrated with fires and light processions.

3. Christ's Ascension
May/Jun (40 days after Easter)
This marks the day that Christ ascended to heaven. In many places, outdoor mass re-enacting the moment of Christ's Ascension takes place.

4. Pentecost
May/Jun (50 days after Easter)
Feast commemorating the Holy Ghost being sent to unite the world's peoples.

5. Corpus Christi
May/Jun (60 days after Easter)
Processions are held and a monstrance is carried from altar to altar.

6. Mary's Ascension
15 Aug
This day commemorates the Virgin Mary's ascension to heaven.

7. All Saints' Day
1 Nov
Austrians visit the graves of their loved ones to light candles and lay wreaths.

8. Feast of the Immaculate Conception
8 Dec
On this day, St Anne conceived a daughter, the Virgin Mary.

9. Christmas Eve
24 Dec
This is the most important day of the festive celebrations, as families gather around the Christmas tree and open presents.

10. Christmas Day
25 Dec
A holy day when people attend church and visit their families.

AREA BY AREA

Aerial view of Central Vienna

CENTRAL VIENNA

With cobbled streets, narrow alleys, quiet squares and a wealth of historic buildings, Vienna's atmospheric heart is brimming with famous landmarks and reminders of both Roman and Habsburg rule. Furthermore, the area is also home to the *crème de la crème* of shops, restaurants and the city's famous cafés and coffee shops. Most of these are located on the three spacious pedestrian zones of Kärntner Strasse, Graben and Kohlmarkt. These streets form an ideal stage for outdoor performers, who entertain summer visitors with music, dance and circus acts. The whole of Central Vienna is a joy to explore, either by strolling its pedestrianized streets or making use of its many bike lanes.

- 1 Top 10 Sights *p95*
- 1 Places to Eat *p103*
- 1 The Best of the Rest *p98*
- 1 Cafés and Tearooms *p102*
- 1 Clubs and Bars *p101*
- 1 Specialist Shops *p99*
- 1 Galleries and Antiques Shops *p100*

For places to stay in this area, see p146

Bronze statue of Prince Eugene in the Hofburg

1 The Hofburg

The former imperial palace *(p26)* may have relinquished its regal position after Austria became a republic in 1918, but the elegance of days gone by is still tangible.

2 Postsparkasse

📍 Q3 🏛 Georg-Coch-Platz 2
🕐 10am–5pm Mon–Fri

In the Postsparkasse building (the post office savings bank), Otto Wagner *(p127)* implemented his principles of combining functionalism with appealing design. Stone panels fixed to the external walls with metal rivets led to the building being nicknamed "a box of nails".

3 Albertina

📍 M5 🏛 Albertinaplatz 1
🕐 10am–6pm daily 🌐 albertina.at 🔗

Once the Habsburgs' residential palace, the Albertina has 20 lavish State Rooms, including the magnificent Hall of Muses and the Rococo Room. Today, it is home to seven major art collections, ranging from contemporary art to graphic, architectural and photographic art, plus period fabrics and costumes. The palace also hosts temporary exhibitions.

4 Ruprechtskirche

📍 N2 🏛 Ruprechtsplatz
🕐 10am–noon & 3–5pm Tue–Fri

This modest church holds the title of Vienna's oldest place of worship. It was built in the 9th century, after the fall of Vindobona, as part of the settlements within the Roman city walls. The stone edifice was the city's main church until the end of the 12th century, when Stephansdom *(p22)* became the most important centre of worship in town. Both east windows date back to the 13th century and have survived the ages untouched as Vienna's oldest works of stained glass.

Ornate Art Nouveau Anker Uhr atop the Uhrbrücke

5 Anker Uhr
🚇 N2 📍 Hoher Markt 10–11

The Anker Uhr clock spans two wings of an insurance company building and was installed between 1911 and 1917 by Austrian sculptor Franz von Matsch. Every day, 12 ornate figures, each symbolizing a period in Vienna's history, step forward on the hour. At noon, all figures parade across the bridge to the tune of music.

6 Burgtheater
🚇 K2 📍 Universitätsring 2 ⏰ 10am–6pm Mon–Fri, 9am–1pm Sat, Sun & public hols 🌐 burgtheater.at 🎭📷

The Burg, as it's called affectionately by the Viennese, was among the first theatres to be built in the German-speaking world. Architects Gottfried Semper and Carl von Hasenauer designed this spectacular building with its Renaissance façade over a period of 14 years (1874–88). A grand staircase with frescoes by Gustav Klimt and his brother Ernst leads from the foyer to the auditorium.

7 Misrachi-Haus
🚇 M2 📍 Judenplatz 8 ⏰ 10am–6pm Sun–Thu, 10am–2pm Fri 🌐 jmw.at 📷

In 2000, during the construction of a Holocaust memorial by

JEWISH VIENNA

Until 1938, most of Vienna's Jewish community lived in Leopoldstadt, an area famous for its theatres, cabarets and synagogues. However, the rise of anti-Semitism under the Nazis led to the decline of the Jewish Quarter. Although many Jewish people have now moved to the nearby Karmeliter quarter, this area still retains its Jewish heritage, with the "city temple" synagogue, vibrant Karmelitermarkt and many kosher restaurants and shops.

British artist Rachel Whiteread on Judenplatz, the archaeological remains of a medieval synagogue were discovered on site. The excavation site is now open to the public and a museum is devoted to the life, work and religion of the city's medieval Jewish community. You can also take a virtual walk around the 15th-century Jewish quarter.

8 Stephansdom

At the geographical epicentre of the city, the spectacular Gothic St Stephen's Cathedral *(p22)* dominates the skyline with its imposing towers and its 137-m- (450-ft-) high spire.

9 Looshaus

🅿 L3 🏛 Michaelerplatz 3
🕐 11:30am–8pm Thu–Sun
🌐 looshaus.at

No other building triggered so much controversy in Vienna as the Looshaus, completed in 1911. Emperor Franz Joseph thought the functional building ruined the square's look and had the curtains closed at his Hofburg palace to avoid looking at it. Four floors are covered in green marble but the building's plain upper floors caused uproar. Today it is home to a restaurant.

10 Pestsäule

🅿 M3 🏛 Graben

The extravagant Baroque Pestsäule (Plague Column) was erected by Habsburg emperor Leopold I in 1679 to commemorate Vienna's deliverance from the horrific plague epidemic that killed more than 100,000 people. Standing on Graben, one of the city's finest shopping boulevards, this 18-m- (70-ft-) tall monument is dedicated to the Holy Trinity. The lavish confection depicts a set of gold-embellished angels and cherubs, symbols of the Trinity, and even the emperor himself.

Beautiful grand staircase in the Burgtheater

A DAY'S STROLL IN CENTRAL VIENNA

Morning

Begin the day at the **Stephansdom** *(p22)*. Catch the sun beaming through the medieval windows, and stroll around the cathedral's Gothic features. Climb the South Tower or take the lift up the North Tower for stunning views over the rooftops. For a break, head to the end of the square and enjoy a cup of tea in **Haas and Haas** *(p99)*.

Wander the web of narrow streets around the cathedral but arrive at Hoher Markt at noon to watch the historic Viennese figures of the **Anker Uhr** march by.

There are many places to have lunch, but on a sunny day pick **DO & CO Stephansplatz** *(p103)* overlooking the cathedral.

Afternoon

Spend the afternoon in **Graben** and **Kohlmarkt**, exploring antiques shops and galleries, until you reach the **Hofburg** palace *(p26)*. Out of its various collections, select those that interest you the most, but don't miss the state apartments where Emperor Franz Joseph lived.

Exit the palace through the huge Michaeler Gate, then pass the **Looshaus**, before enjoying a slice of *Sachertorte* at **Café Demel** *(p102)*.

Finally, if you're visiting in winter, take tram 1 going clockwise from **Karlsplatz** to **Schwedenplatz** to see the floodlit buildings by night.

The Best of the Rest

**Baroque façade of
the Peterskirche**

1. Franziskanerplatz

N4

This charming square is home to
the Franziskanerkirche, pretty houses
and the Moses fountain (1798).

2. Altes Rathaus

N2 Wipplingerstrasse 8
To the public

The Habsburgs confiscated this palace
in 1316 from the German brothers
Otto and Haymo of Neuburg, who
had conspired against them. It func-
tioned as the town hall until 1883.

3. Kirche am Hof

M2 Am Hof 7 10am–6pm
Mon–Sat, 1–6pm Sun

Emperor Ferdinand III's widow had this
church built in 1662. It is more reminis-
cent of a palace than a place of worship.

4. Akademie der Wissenschaften

P3 Dr-Ignaz-Seipel-Platz 2
This ornate Rococo building (1755)
was formerly the site of Vienna
University. The Academy of Sciences
hall staged the premiere of Joseph
Haydn's (p66) The Creation in 1808.

5. Peterskirche

M3 Petersplatz 8am–
7pm Mon–Fri, 9am–7pm Sat &
Sun petershirche.at

This Baroque church has a dramatic
and ornate high altar and exquisite
frescoes by Johann Michael Rottmayr.

6. Heiligenkreuzerhof

P3

A tranquil courtyard featuring a set
of 17th- and 18th-century apartment
buildings and a medieval chapel.

7. Memorial against War and Fascism

M5 Albertinaplatz,
Augustinerstrasse 8

Artist Alfred Hrdlicka's powerful
sculpture memorializes World War II
and the atrocities of Nazi governance
that led to the death of nearly 65,000
Viennese Jews in concentration camps.

8. Börse

L1 Schottenring 16
Once the home of the Vienna Stock
Exchange, this building, designed by
Danish architect Theophil von Hansen,
is now used by the government.

9. Kapuzinerkirche

M4 Neuer Markt 10am–6pm
daily wien.hapuziner.at

The simple design of this church is in
line with the Capuchin order's doctrine.
Emperor Matthias established a crypt
(p68) for the Habsburgs here.

10. Minoritenkirche

L3 Minoritenplatz 2
minoritenkirche.wien

When Duke Leopold VI returned
safely from a crusade in 1219, he
built a church on this site. Its medieval character is still visible.

Specialist Shops

1. Haas and Haas
N3 🏠 Stephansplatz 4
🌐 haas-haas.at
Just behind Stephansdom, this shop offers more than 200 assorted fruit teas, black teas, herbal teas and many tea accessories. The marzipan sweets and chocolates are divine.

2. Xocolat
L2 🏠 Freyung 2, in the Palais Ferstel 🌐 xocolat.at
Everything in this little shop revolves around chocolate, with more than 120 varieties from all over the world, as well as books on the subject.

3. Doblinger
M4 🏠 Dorotheergasse 10
🌐 doblinger.at
This music publishing house has every music score a musician can dream of. Be it classical or contemporary music, Doblinger has it all.

4. Mayr and Fessler
N4 🏠 Kärntner Strasse 37
🌐 mayr-fessler.at
Mayr and Fessler is a great place for top-of-the-range fountain pens, as well as diaries and organizers. It has a range of Italian writing and wrapping paper as well as notebooks and accessories.

5. Gmundner Ceramics
D2 🏠 Stadiongasse 7
🌐 gmundnerkeramikshop.at
Pretty Austrian hand-painted pottery is produced at Gmunden in Upper Austria. The traditional decoration of green-on-white looks sloshed-on, but perfect. This shop offers a range of wares and patterns just outside the Ring behind Parliament.

6. Shakespeare and Co
N2 🏠 Sterngasse 2
🌐 shakespeare.co.at
This tiny bookshop is brimming with character and is the best place to go for contemporary English literature. There are also very good travel and poetry sections.

7. Knize
M3 🏠 Graben 13 🌐 knize.at
Founded by Bohemian tailor Josef Kniže, this internationally admired establishment is known for its bespoke suits.

8. Loden Plankl
L3 🏠 Michaelerplatz 6
🌐 loden-plankl.at
This place offers traditional Austrian clothing ranging from Loden coats and jackets to Dirndl dresses and Lederhosen (leather trousers).

9. Augarten Flagship Store
M4 🏠 Spiegelgasse 3
🌐 augarten.com
The porcelain at the city outlet of Vienna's historic factory ranges from fine tableware to Wiener Werkstätte designs and modern objets d'art.

10. Meinl am Graben
M3 🏠 Am Graben 19
🌐 meinlamgraben.eu
One of Vienna's best delicatessens, this spot has a great selection of chocolates, dessert wines, coffee and fresh produce.

Assortment of goodies at Meinl am Graben

Galleries and Antiques Shops

1. Dorotheum Auction House
M4 **Dorotheergasse 17**
dorotheum.at
Vienna is well known for its antiques, and Dorotheergasse is one of the main areas to head for if this is your interest. At the city's main auction house, in operation since 1907, you can buy everything from antique furniture to jewellery and paintings.

2. Alte Kunst und Militaria
M4 **Plankengasse 7**
militaria-hoech.at
Books, guns, sabers, medals and old uniforms from past military campaigns are stocked here.

3. Wissenschaftliches Kabinett
M4 **Spiegelgasse 23**
wisshab.com
This is a fascinating place to browse for unique objects such as antique surgical saws, phrenology skulls and chess pieces.

4. Sonja Reisch
M3 **Bräunerstrasse 10**
antiquitaeten-reisch.com
Silver- and tableware, along with jewellery, glass and decorative objects from the Biedermeier era, are sold here.

Vintage teddy bears on display at the Galerie Ambiente

5. Antiquariat Inlibris
J3 **Rathausstrasse 19**
inlibris.at
Scientific books, early prints and Austrian memorabilia are just some of the specialities at this antiquarian bookshop, established in 1883.

6. Peter Kulcsar
M4 **Spiegelgasse 19** **kulcsar.at**
One of the longest-established antique shops in Vienna, Peter Kulcsar sells a wide selection of interesting curios and furniture dating from the 16th to the 20th centuries.

7. Galerie Hofstätter
M4 **Bräunerstrasse 7**
galerie-hofstaetter.com
This gallery organizes exhibitions all year round, with a focus on Austrian post-war and contemporary art.

8. Galerie Hilger
M4 **Dorotheergasse 5**
hilger.at
Artworks from the early 20th century, as well as works by contemporary Austrian and international artists, are showcased as part of nine annual exhibitions.

9. Galerie Charim
M4 **Dorotheergasse 12**
charimgalerie.at
This gallery in the former Palais Gatterburg specializes in Austrian art, including object art and new media, as well as photography.

10. Galerie Ambiente
N3 **Lugech 1** **ambiente galerieambiente.at**
Beautiful and innovative furniture, from Viennese designers and manufacturers such as Josef Hoffmann and Thonet, is sold at Ambiente. The shop also has a collection of vintage teddy bears. They can also arrange shipping to get your goods sent directly home.

Stylish rooftop interior of Skybar

Clubs and Bars

1. American Bar
N4 **Kärntner Passage**
loosbar.at
Set in a simple yet sophisticated Adolf Loos building, this bar is one of the most beautiful night-spots in town. It serves delicious cocktails.

2. Planter's Club
C4 **Zelinkagasse 4**
plantersclub.com
This historical bar, with its teak wood panelling, evokes a tea plantation house. You can choose from more than 300 whiskies, 90 rums and many mouthwatering cocktails.

3. Bermuda Bräu
P2 **Rabensteig 6**
bermuda-braeu.at
Located in a hip area called the Bermuda Triangle, this lively pub offers superb draught beer served in clay jugs, as well as a variety of bottled beers. It has a dance floor in the basement.

4. Palmenhaus
This renovated imperial greenhouse hosts a stylish restaurant (p103) and bar with fine Austrian wines and occasional live DJ nights.

5. Volksgarten
K4 **Burgring 1** **volksgarten.at**
The Volksgarten is one of the city's most established party zones, with a varied mix of music. The fabulous garden is an ideal setting in summer.

6. Onyx Bar
N3 **Haas-Haus, Stephansplatz 12, 7th floor** **docohotel.com**
Vienna's in-crowd gathers in this bar with its fine view of Stephansdom (p22). Snacks, cocktails and groovy background music are on offer.

7. Meinz
N2 **Seitenstettengasse 5**
meinz.wien
Soak up some live jazz, blues, soul and modern music while sipping on creative cocktails at this intimate bar.

8. Jazzland
N2 **Franz-Josefs-Kai 29**
jazzland.at
Housed in a 500-year-old cellar, this venue is the oldest jazz club in Austria.

9. Roter Engel
P2 **Rabensteig 5** **roterengel.at**
Music is the speciality of this bar, with local artists playing rock, pop, funk and soul every Monday to Thursday.

10. Skybar
N4 **Kärntner Strasse 19**
steffl-vienna.at
Located inside the department store Steffl, this bar has a great vibe and a view over Vienna's rooftops. The cocktails are excellent.

Cafés and Tearooms

1. Café Demel
M3 ⬡ Kohlmarkt 14 ⬡ demel.com
An opulent interior and central location make Demel an ideal rest stop for pastries and other snacks.

2. Café Hawelka
M3 ⬡ Dorotheergasse 6
⬡ hawelka.at
Open until 1am on weekends, Café Hawelka features old-world decor. It's famous for its coffee, cakes and sweet rolls.

3. Café Diglas
P2 ⬡ Fleischmarkt 16
⬡ fleischmarkt.diglas.at
A charming café, Diglas sells delicious cakes, and you can even watch some being made in its historic bakery.

4. L. Heiner K.u.K. Hofzuckerbäcker
N4 ⬡ Kärntner Strasse 21–23
⬡ heiner.co.at
This branch of the six Heiner cafés serves excellent marzipan and flaky pastries.

5. Café Landtmann
K2 ⬡ Universitätsring 4
⬡ landtmann.at
A temple to the traditional concept of a coffee house, with service and prices to match. There's a small terrace for dining alfresco.

6. Café Bräunerhof
M4 ⬡ Stallburggasse 2 ⬡ 01 512 38 93
Featuring live classical music on Saturdays, this place is traditional but simple in style.

7. Kurkonditorei OBERLAA
M4 ⬡ Neuer Markt 16
⬡ oberlaa-wien.at
Kurkonditorei OBERLAA is known for its desserts. In the summer, you can enjoy a cup of coffee in the square outside.

8. Café Prückel
Q3 ⬡ Stubenring 24 ⬡ prueckel.at
A reworking of the traditional coffee house in 1950s retro design, Prückel is near MAK, the Museum of Applied Arts (mak.at).

9. Café Korb
M3 ⬡ Brandstätte 9 ⬡ cafekorb.at
Tuck into tasty apple strudel at this café. The Art Lounge in its basement organizes art, music, drama and literary events.

10. Café Central
L2 ⬡ Herrengasse 14
⬡ cafecentral.wien
This café modestly claims to be the "true centre" of Vienna, with an interior that features lofty vaulted ceilings.

Patrons enjoying alfresco dining at Café Demel

Places to Eat

Modern interior of Italian restaurant Fabios

PRICE CATEGORIES
For a three-course meal for one with half a bottle of wine (or equivalent meal), taxes and extra charges.

€ under €35 €€ €35–70 €€€ over €70

1. Restaurant in Hotel Ambassador

N4 **Kärntnerstrasse 22** **ambassador.at · €€**

A menu ranging from traditional favourites to fish and meat dishes is served here.

2. Steirereck

Q4 **Am Heumarkt 2A, Stadtpark** **Sat & Sun** **steirereck.at · €€€**

The highly rated Steirereck makes for an essential dining experience.

3. Fabios

M3 **Tuchlauben 6** **fabios.at · €€€**

This sleek Italian restaurant is frequented by Vienna's glitterati and is one of the city's trendiest dining spots.

4. Palmenhaus

M5 **Burggarten 1** **palmenhaus.at · €€**

This Art Nouveau conservatory offers great views and good food. There's also dancing on weekend evenings.

5. DO & CO Stephansplatz

N3 **Haas Haus, Stephansplatz 12** **docohotel.com · €€€**

This stylish rooftop venue offers a sophisticated selection of the best dishes from around the world.

6. Silvio Nickol

P4 **Palais Coburg, Coburgbastei 4** **palais-coburg.com · €€€**

Famous for its tasting menus, the Michelin-starred Silvio Nickol serves exquisite contemporary fare.

7. Plachutta

N3 **Wollzeile 38** **plachutta.at · €€**

This traditional Viennese place is known for its beef dishes. Don't miss the *tafelspitz* with roasted potatoes.

8. Wrenkh

N3 **Bauernmarkt 10** **Sun & hols** **wrenkh-wien.at · €**

Wrenkh is one of the most popular vegetarian restaurants in the city.

9. Zum Schwarzen Kameel

M3 **Bognerstrasse 5** **schwarzeshameel.at · €€**

This quaint restaurant serves delicious traditional dishes as well as international cuisines.

10. Stadtbeisl Inigo

P3 **Bächerstrasse 18** **inigo.at · €**

Viennese and international cuisine. Wine list changes every other month.

Chef preparing for service at DO & CO Stephansplatz

SCHOTTENRING AND ALSERGRUND

A large part of this area is inhabited by medical institutions, including the AKH general hospital, the Josephinum and the Vienna medical school. This is perhaps not surprising for the place where the psychoanalyst Sigmund Freud lived and worked in the early 20th century. Besides these institutions, the area also features some sights with historical significance and exceptional natural beauty. Highlights include the Voltivkirche, with its imposing façade; the Sigmund Freud Park, a favourite spot with students in summer; and the elegant double staircase of the Strudlhofstiege, which looks like its straight out of a film.

1 Top 10 Sights
p105

1 Places to Eat
p109

1 Student Hangouts
p108

For places to stay in this area, see p147

Art Nouveau Strudlhofstiege staircase by Theodor Jäger

1 Strudlhofstiege
B3 **Strudlhofgasse to Liechtensteinstrasse**

This striking Art Nouveau outdoor double staircase, which winds its way down from Strudlhofgasse to Liechtensteinstrasse, was designed by Austrian architect Theodor Jäger in 1910. Two fountains, several lampposts and various ramps create a graceful impression. It became famous in 1951, when Austrian writer Heimito von Doderer published a novel named after the stairway.

2 Rossauer Kaserne
B4 **Schlickplatz 6**
To the public

These huge barracks were created to protect Vienna from attacks from outside the city, as well as revolt from within, after the revolutions that took place across Europe in 1848. Together with two other military camps, the Rossauer base formed a strategic triangle. Work on

Memorial at the Rossauer Kaserne

the barracks began in 1864 and was completed six years later. They became the city's police headquarters after World War II.

3 Gartenpalais Liechtenstein
A3 **Fürstengasse 1**
w palaisliechtenstein.com

Built as the summer residence for the Liechtenstein family at the end of the 17th century, the Liechtenstein Garden Palace is Vienna's premier home of Baroque art. The collection includes works by many important artists, such as Raphael, Rubens and Rembrandt. The lovely formal gardens are free and open to the public. Guided tours in English are available on Saturdays; check the website for details.

4 Servitenkirche
B3 **Servitengasse 9**
9am–10pm daily

Although this church is slightly off the beaten track, it is well worth a visit. Built by the Servite convent along with an adjoining monastery in 1651, the interior is decorated with stucco ornaments and frescoes, but the most interesting detail is the 13th-century crucifix to the right of the high altar. Originally the "cross of gallows", it stood at the public execution place on Schlickplatz.

5 Votivkirche

📍 C3 📌 Rooseveltplatz
🕐 10am–6pm Tue–Fri, 11am–7pm Sat,
9am–1pm Sun 🌐 votivkirche.at 🚻♿

This striking church is part of
the Ringstrasse. Inside, there is
a museum with jewelled chalices
and other sacred objects. Holy Mass
is conducted every second Saturday
at 11:15am in multiple languages.

6 Josephinum

📍 B3 📌 Währinger Strasse 25
🕐 Hours vary, check website
🌐 josephinum.ac.at ♿

Founded by Emperor Joseph II
in 1785, the Josephinum was a
medical academy where military
doctors and general practitioners
trained. Today, it houses the Institute
for the History of Medicine. Book
ahead for tours in English.

7 Vienna University

📍 K1 📌 Universitätsring 1
🕐 6am–10pm Mon–Fri, 7am–
7pm Sat 🌐 univie.ac.at ♿

The university was founded by Duke
Rudolf IV in 1365. The present building
was constructed in Italian Renaissance
style on a former army parade ground
following plans by Austrian architect
Heinrich Ferstel, and opened in 1884.
From the entrance hall with marble
columns, grand staircases lead to the
lecture theatres and the library. The
arcaded courtyard is lined with busts

of distinguished professors and the
university's eight Nobel Prize winners.
The ceremony hall is decorated with
frescoes (1895) by Gustav Klimt.

SIGMUND FREUD

In his study of the unconscious
mind, Sigmund Freud (1856–1939)
divided the human psyche into
three levels (id, ego and superego)
that, if unbalanced, could cause
mental disorder. His ideas were
the foundation of modern psychoanalysis. Anna Freud, his daughter,
followed in his footsteps and
is considered the founder of
child psychoanalysis.

---

8 Sigmund Freud Museum

📍 B3 📌 Berggasse 19
🕐 10am–6pm Wed–Mon
🌐 freud-museum.at ♿

The founder of psychoanalysis lived in
Vienna from 1891 until 1938, when he
fled from the National Socialists to
London. In his spacious apartment in
Berggasse, now a museum, he wrote
many famous works and case histories
such as *The Interpretation of Dreams*.

Neo-Gothic interior
of the Votivkirche

A DAY IN VIENNA'S STUDENT DISTRICT

Morning

Start your day at **Vienna University**, exploring the marble entrance hall and the courtyard. Then head towards the beautiful **Votivkirche**. Walk up Alser Strasse until you reach the **Altes Allgemeines Krankenhaus**, the former general hospital. For a break, head to one of the pubs in the large first courtyard.

Head to courtyard 13, where the **Pathologisch-Anatomisches Museum** (p61) is situated. Cut your way to **Strudlhofgasse** and stride down **Strudlhofstiege** (p105), where you can spot the **Gartenpalais Liechtenstein** (p105). In **Porzellangasse** you will find several places for lunch.

Afternoon

On your way to the **Sigmund Freud Museum**, pass by **Servitenkirche** (p105) and stop for a glimpse of the Baroque interior. Browse around Dr Freud's apartment and consulting rooms. For a quick cup of coffee, **Florentin 1090** (p108) just across the road is a great spot. Later, spend a while people-watching in the **Sigmund Freud Park** (p108), a popular hangout.

You can round the day off with a visit to **Votiv Kino** (votivkino.at), an arts cinema that shows independent films in the original language.

9 Schubert's House of Birth

A2 ⧉ Nussdorfer Strasse 54 🕑 10am–1pm & 2–6pm Tue–Sun & public hols ↻

Franz Schubert (p66) was born in the kitchen of this little first-floor apartment, now a museum, on 31 January 1797 and spent the first four years of his life in the property, known locally as "House of the Red Crab". The museum has information on the composer's life as well as portraits by Schubert's contemporaries.

10 Altes Allgemeines Krankenhaus

B2 ⧉ Spitalgasse 2 🖥 univie.ac.at

This sprawling former hospital complex with 11 courtyards is a beautiful oasis of calm. In the late 18th century, Emperor Joseph II converted an existing house for the poor into a general hospital, which included a "birth house", a "foundling house", and a "mad house" – today a pathological museum (p61). The complex is now part of the Vienna University campus.

Relaxing on the grassy lawn at Sigmund Freud Park

Student Hangouts

1. Stiegl-Ambulanz

C2 University Campus, Alser Strasse 4 stiegl-ambulanz.com

Open all year round, Stiegl-Ambulanz offers traditional Viennese food at reasonable prices. It also has a wide range of beers.

2. Florentin 1090

C3 Berggasse 8 florentin1090.com

A trendy hangout next door to the LGBTQ+ bookshop Löwenherz, serving tasty Middle Eastern and Austrian dishes.

3. Cafeteria Maximilian

K1 Universitätsstrasse 2 01 405 7149

Right by Vienna University (p106), this cafeteria serves simple comfort food, attracting hordes of people, many of whom stay a while to socialize.

4. Statt-Beisl in the WUK

B2 Währinger Strasse 59 statt-beisl.info

This former 19th-century locomotive factory has been cleverly converted into a cultural centre and operates a café and restaurant.

5. Juice Factory

C3 Schottengasse 4 juicefactory.at

The natural fruit and vegetable concoctions at this juice bar help to refresh and detox. Coffee and smoothie breakfast bowls are also offered.

6. Sigmund Freud Park

K1

On a sunny day, these verdant lawns are inhabited by students studying, picnicking, sunbathing and debating the issues of the day.

7. Charlie P's

C3 Währinger Strasse 3 charlieps.at

A traditional Irish pub, Charlie P's has a particularly lively atmosphere. Fish and chips and Guinness are essential parts of the menu.

8. Gangl

C2 University Campus, Alser Strasse 4 gangl.at

Beer on tap, toasted sandwiches and a cosy atmosphere (as well as seating outside in summer) attract a loyal crowd of students here.

9. Café Stein

C3 Währinger Strasse 6–8 cafestein.at

This spot has seating inside and out, and offers a good view of the nearby Votivkirche (p106). This is a great choice for a traditional breakfast, and it also hosts various cultural events.

10. Café Votiv

C3 Währinger Strasse 12 votivkino.at

The trendy café within the Votiv cinema is popular with students as well as, of course, cinemagoers before and after film screenings.

Places to Eat

PRICE CATEGORIES

For a three-course meal for one with half a bottle of wine (or equivalent meal), taxes and extra charges.

€ under €35 €€ €35–70 €€€ over €70

1. Kim Kocht
C3 Währinger Strasse 46 D Mon & Tue; Sat & Sun kimkocht · €€€

Celebrity chef Sohyi Kim runs this trendy venue, serving Korean-fusion cuisine with mostly fish, seafood and vegetarian dishes.

2. Roter Löwenhof
J1 Rotenlöwengasse 17 Mon & Tue roterloewenhof.at · €€

Traditional and modern at the same time, the Red Lion serves up Viennese classics, hearty desserts and Austrian wines.

3. Café Weimar
B2 Währinger Strasse 68 cafeweimar.at · €

Established in 1900, this traditional café-restaurant serves hot and cold snacks and offers a set lunch at midday. There's live piano music with operetta and jazz tunes.

4. D'Landsknecht
B3 Porzellangasse 13 landsknecht.at · €

A long-established local favourite: expect hearty portions of traditional Austrian soups and main dishes at moderate prices here.

5. Restaurant Roth
B3 Währinger Strasse 1 roth.or.at · €

Designed to resemble an American diner, this one-of-a-kind restaurant in Hotel Regina serves excellent Austrian and Viennese fare. You can enjoy your meal inside or in the garden.

6. Oasia
B4 Schlickgasse 2 Sun oasia-restaurant.at · €

Dim sum is a speciality at this modern Asian-fusion restaurant.

7. Der Wiener Deewan
C3 Liechtensteinstrasse 10 Sun & public hols deewan.at · €€

The Pakistani menu served here has garnered rave reviews. You can also indulge in the all-you-can-eat buffet.

8. Suppenwirtschaft
B3 Servitengasse 6 D Mon–Fri; Sat, Sun & public hols suppenwirtschaft.at · €

This vegan-friendly restaurant offers a seasonal menu of soups, salads and curries. Takeaway is the norm here, as the seating area is small.

9. Ragusa
B3 Berggasse 15 Sun ragusa.at · €€

Dalmatian cooking (specialities include fish and seafood) in a cosy atmosphere with outdoor seating.

10. Stomach
B3 Seegasse 26 01 310 20 99 Mon & Tue · €€

Enjoy modern food in one of the nicest outdoor dining areas.

Diners enjoying a meal in the courtyard of Stomach

MUSEUMSQUARTIER, TOWN HALL AND NEUBAU

The areas around the MuseumsQuartier, Town Hall and Neubau represent both the political centre of Austria and the cultural heart of the capital, being home to a mix of government bureaus, world-class exhibition spaces and funky, Bohemian boutiques in lively, character-packed cobbled streets. This is where conventional Vienna and the city's edgier, arty side meet among restaurants, shops, vintage stores, museums and galleries. The Kunsthistorisches and Naturhistorisches museums hold Habsburg treasures beyond compare, and the modern MuseumsQuartier is a lively hub of contemporary art. To the west, Spittelberg's streets are among the most picturesque and atmospheric in all Vienna.

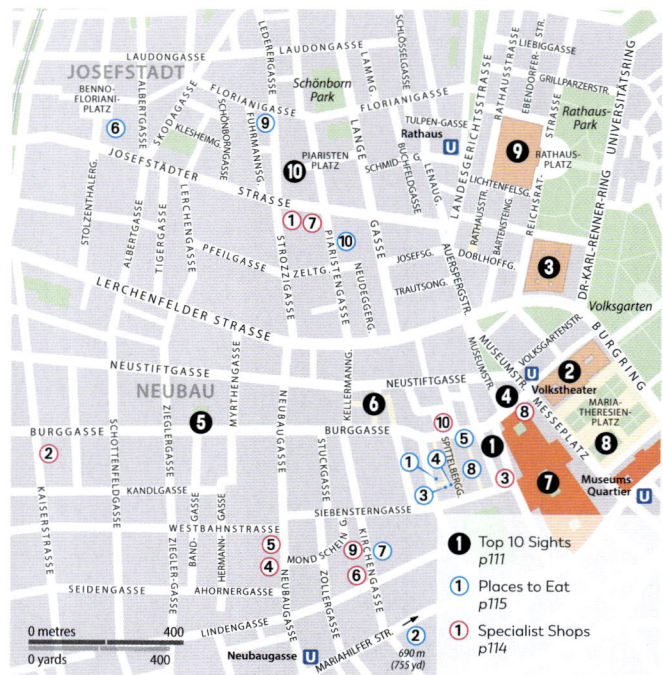

1 Top 10 Sights *p111*

1 Places to Eat *p115*

1 Specialist Shops *p114*

For places to stay in this area, see p147

1 Spittelberg
J5

The charming Spittelberg area consists of a few cobbled, narrow streets with pretty houses and spouting fountains between Breite Gasse, Siebensterngasse, Sigmundsgasse and Burggasse. In the 18th century, the area was full of hovels, gambling dens and brothels, but by the 19th century these had been closed down and, over time, the district became increasingly derelict. The city authorities only began to recognize the area's charm in the 1970s, and today it's a thriving enclave of galleries, handicraft shops and cosy pubs.

2 Naturhistorisches Museum
K4 **Maria-Theresienplatz**
9am–6:30pm Thu–Mon, 9am–8pm Wed **nhm-wien.ac.at**

Often voted among the world's top ten museums and built as a mirror image of its more famous neighbour, the Kunsthistorisches Museum, the Natural History Museum opened in 1889. The collections of archaeology, natural history and geology grew out of Emperor Franz Stephan's 1748 collection of natural curiosities. The museum's interior was designed to enhance the exhibits, which number more than 20 million. The most precious rarities are the 25,000-year-old Venus of Willendorf figurine and a "bouquet of jewels" given to Francis I by his wife Maria Theresa.

Fountain in the grounds of the Naturhistorisches Museum

Greek theatre-style Federal Assembly Hall of the Parliament

3 Parliament
K3 **Dr-Karl-Renner-Ring 3** **parlament.gv.at**

This building (1873–83) was designed by the architect Theophil von Hansen in Greek style to celebrate the cradle of democracy. Two ramps lined by statues of Greek philosophers lead to the main entrance. The first Austrian Republic was declared here in 1918. Visitors are required to register on the website ahead of their visit.

4 Volkstheater
J4 **Arthur-Schnitzler-Platz 1** **volkstheater.at**

The Volkstheater ("people's theatre") was established in 1889 as a counterpart to the imperial Burgtheater *(p96)*. Its aim was to offer classic and modern drama to a larger audience at reasonable prices. Constructed by the acclaimed architects Ferdinand Fellner and Hermann Helmer, this theatre was designed in Historicist style and fitted with the latest technology of the time, such as electric lighting. With just under 1,000 seats, it is among the largest German-language theatres in the world.

5 Neubau
C2

The Neubau district attracts a steady stream of hipster tourists to studios, cool cafés, vintage clothes boutiques and independent stores. In the last decade, Neubau's arty, progressive character has emerged as "Vienna's Berlin". A leisurely stroll around the galleries and kooky outlets in its backstreets gives visitors a chance to experience the city's alternative side. An eclectic mishmash of shops sells everything from modern textiles, eco-fashion bespoke jewellery and fetish gear to gourmet foods, bizarre kitchen gadgets, photographic art and multicoloured retro frocks. Fanning north from the Mariahilfer Strasse towards the Lerchenfelder Strasse, Neubau's stores run along Neubaugasse and Lindengasse. The MuseumsQuartier marks the district's eastern border.

RINGSTRASSE

The Ringstrasse encircles the city's first district and is one of the world's most elegant avenues. In 1857 Franz Joseph I ordered Vienna's medieval strongholds be torn down and the city be given an imperial face with grand edifices. Palaces were then built along the new boulevard that was officially opened in 1865.

6 Sankt-Ulrichs-Platz
E2

At the heart of this charming cobbled square is St Ulrich's Church, which is surrounded by a pretty ensemble of patrician houses dating back to various periods. At No. 5 is a rare example of a Renaissance house, while the Baroque edifice at No. 27 bears a statue of St Nepomuk, who gave the house its name. During the Turkish Siege of 1683, Kara Mustafa's troops pitched their tents on this square.

7 MuseumsQuartier

The former imperial stables have been imaginatively transformed into a vast complex of museums and entertainment venues (p42) that shouldn't be missed.

8 Kunsthistorisches Museum

Vienna's Kunsthistorisches Museum (p32) is home to an impressive collection of artistic treasures, spanning the centuries from the ancient world to the modern day. Its sumptuous galleries also feature an excellent array of Old Masters – here you'll find the world's largest collection of Bruegels alongside Giuseppe Arcimboldo's curious portraits composed from fruit and vegetables, and works by Rembrandt, Caravaggio, Titian and Holbein.

Distinctive spires of the Neues Rathaus

9 Neues Rathaus

📍 J2 🏛 Friedrich-Schmidt-Platz 1
🌐 wien.gv.at

The Neo-Gothic town hall, with its spires, loggias and stone rosettes in the pointed windows, was built by Friedrich von Schmidt in 1883 to express the inhabitants' pride in their city at that time. The impressive building has seven arcaded courtyards and 1,575 rooms, where the Vienna City Council and the mayor have their offices. All year round, various festivals take place on the square in front of the Rathaus, ranging from a Christmas market to a music film festival *(p90)* in summer. The building's façade is spectacularly highlighted at night by floodlights. Tours with audio guides in English are available from 1pm onwards on Monday, Wednesday and Friday.

10 Piaristenkirche Maria Treu

📍 D2 🏛 Jodok Fink Platz ⏰ During church services 🌐 mariatreu.at

Walking into narrow Piaristengasse from Josefstädter Strasse, the charming square on the left comes as a surprise. The Piaristenkirche Maria Treu (Maria Treu Church) here was built from 1719 onwards to a design by Lukas von Hildebrandt. The dome's frescoes are by the Austrian Baroque artist Franz Anton Maulbertsch (1752). The column in front of the church was installed in 1713 to give thanks for the end of a plague epidemic.

The Triumphal Procession of Bacchus,
Kunsthistorisches Museum

A WALK AROUND THE MUSEUMSQUARTIER

Morning

Begin your day at the **Neues Rathaus**, then stroll along the Ringstrasse towards **Parliament** *(p111)*. Once you've taken in these political gems, you can then explore the city's wonderful museums.

The museum highlights are the **Kunsthistorisches Museum** *(p32)* and **Naturhistorisches Museum** *(p111)*, and you could easily spend a full day in each of them, so be sure to select your main areas of interest and concentrate on those collections. Enjoy a cup of coffee in the museums themselves – the cafés in both are excellent.

Walk across the square to the **MuseumsQuartier** and wander around the many courtyards. Stop for lunch in any of the four excellent restaurants in the complex.

Afternoon

After lunch, visit **mumok** *(p43)* and the **Leopold Museum** *(p42)*, before leaving the complex through gates 6 or 7. Either leads you straight to the **Volkstheater** *(p111)*. Make your way up Burggasse and the **Spittelberg** area *(p111)* spills out to your left, where you can look around the shops and galleries.

After dark, return to the Neues Rathaus to see it lit up against the night sky.

Specialist Shops

1. Quendler's feine Weine
🅟 D2 🏠 Josefstädter Strasse 33
🅦 quendler.at
This is the top spot in Vienna for fine red and white Austrian wines, as well as wines from around the world.

2. Grand Cru
🅟 E2 🏠 Kaiserstrasse 67
🅦 grandcru.at
Choose from a great selection of coffees, as well as delicious chocolates with various tasty fillings here.

3. Teehaus Artee
🅟 E2 🏠 Siebensterngasse 4
🅦 artee.at
Offering a range of teas along with stylish teapots and cups, Artee is an elegant spot to buy and sample tea. Asian food is also served here.

4. Ina Kent Store
🅟 E2 🏠 Neubaugasse 34
🅦 inakent.com
A specialist in leather goods, including handbags, this store also hosts changing exhibitions in the shop.

5. Mastnak
🅟 E2 🏠 Neubaugasse 31
🅦 mastnak.at
One of two shops, stocking everything from drawing pencils to schoolbags and wrapping paper. It also does printing and copying.

Baked treats on sale at Grand Cru

Stylish furniture and homeware at Das Möbel

6. Geschirr Niessner
🅟 E2 🏠 Kirchengasse 9A
🅦 geschirr-wien.at
This kitchen equipment emporium has plenty of vintage products, such as English and Austrian porcelain.

7. Vinoe
🅟 D2 🏠 Piaristengasse 35 🅦 vinoe.at
The specialist in wines from Lower Austria stocks 400 varieties.

8. Combinat
🅟 J4 🏠 Museumsplatz 1
🅦 combinat.at
Located in the Leopold Museum, this small store sells a wide range of clothes, bags and other fashion items from Austrian designers.

9. ZERUM
🅟 F2 🏠 Kirchengasse 13 🅦 zerum.store
ZERUM offers men's, women's and children's fashion with a great sustainable twist.

10. Das Möbel
🅟 E2 🏠 Burggasse 10
🅦 cafe.dasmoebel.at
A mixture between a furniture gallery, café and restaurant where you can shop while having a drink or a meal.

Places to Eat

1. Amerling Beisl
📍 E2 🏠 Stiftgasse 8
🌐 amerlingbeisl.at · €
This Biedermeier-style courtyard garden, open in summer, serves Viennese comfort food, including noodles and dumplings.

2. Market
📍 F3 🏠 Linke Wienzeile 36
🌐 market-restaurant.at · €€
This Asian restaurant with a striking interior and an upmarket vibe offers excellent Japanese-inspired dishes.

3. Plutzer Bräu
📍 E2 🏠 Schrankgasse 2
🌐 plutzerbraeu.at · €
A pub serving burgers, with huge TV screens for sports fans. In summer there is seating outside.

4. Tian Bistro
📍 E2 🏠 Schrankgasse 4
🌐 tian-bistro.com · €€
The shaded gardens here provide respite on hot days and it's an oasis for vegetarians in meat-eating Vienna.

5. Zu ebener Erde und erster Stock
📍 E2 🏠 Burggasse 13 🕐 Sat & Sun 🌐 zu-ebener-erde-und-erster-stoch.at · €€
On the ground and first floors of a Biedermeier-style house, this restaurant serves creative and traditional Austrian cuisine and fine wines.

6. Prinz Ferdinand
📍 D1 🏠 Bennoplatz 2 🌐 prinzferdinand.gusti.at · €€
A typical Viennese restaurant serving Austrian specialities, with romantic seating underneath trees on the square.

7. Figar
📍 E2 🏠 Kirchengasse 18 🕐 Thu 🌐 figar.net · €
Excellent brunches and several vegetarian options are offered here.

PRICE CATEGORIES
For a three-course meal for one with half a bottle of wine (or equivalent meal), taxes and extra charges.
....
€ under €35   €€ €35–70   €€€ over €70

Figar is something of a hipster hangout. It is open until 2am and there is a pleasant outdoor patio in summer.

8. Witwe Bolte
📍 J5 🏠 Gutenberggasse 13
🕐 L Mon–Fri 🌐 witwebolte.at · €€
This cosy spot in the Spittelberg area has outdoor seating in summer, a delightful interior and offers refined Viennese cuisine and Austrian wines.

9. Tunnel
📍 D1 🏠 Florianigasse 39
🌐 tunnel-vienna-live.at · €
A mix of international food and plenty of Asian dishes feature on the menu here. In the evenings, there is live music until it closes at 2am.

10. Ilija
📍 D2 🏠 Piaristengasse 36
🕐 Sun 🌐 ilija.at · €€
Cosy Croatian restaurant serves seasonal dishes, fish and other specialities from the Dalmatian coast.

Diners enjoying a meal at Tunnel

Clockwise from left
Piaristenkirche Maria Treu: the church's dome; its ornate façade; a statue of the Virgin Mary on the column outside the church

OPERA AND NASCHMARKT

This is a multifaceted area, which features a number of architectural landmarks standing regally alongside the colourful activity of the Naschmarkt. It is characterized by great buildings of various styles such as the historic State Opera House and the Academy of Fine Arts, as well as the finest examples of Viennese Art Nouveau with the Secession Building and two stunning Otto Wagner houses on Linke Wienzeile. The area is also a shoppers' paradise – Mariahilfer Strasse, the longest shopping street in Vienna, has hundreds of stores and many cafés and restaurants. Meanwhile, the Naschmarkt offers a different kind of retail experience, with its lively market bearing some resemblance to Middle Eastern bazaars and providing a delight for all the senses.

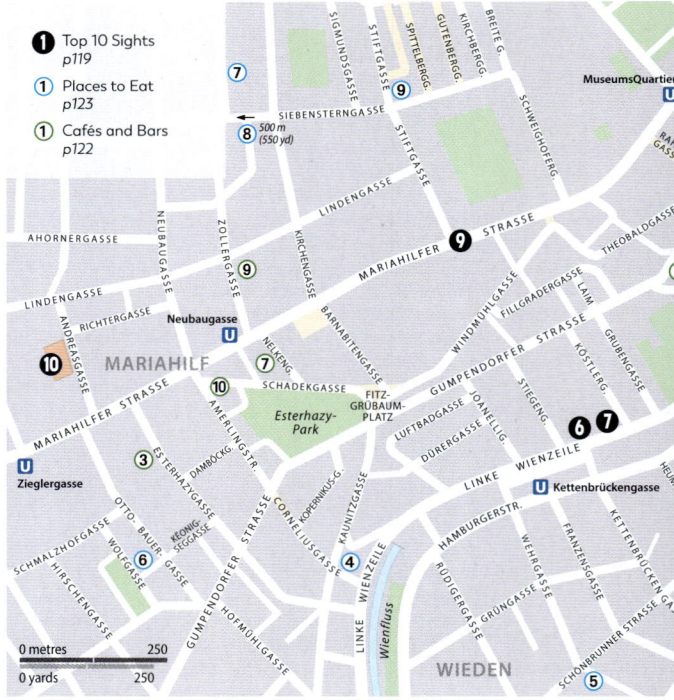

① Top 10 Sights
p119

① Places to Eat
p123

① Cafés and Bars
p122

For places to stay in this area, see p148

Paintings in the Akademie der bildenden Künste Art Collections

1 Staatsoper

The Vienna State Opera House *(p44)* is an iconic landmark in a city that is passionate about its music. Its 300 performances a year attract an international audience, as does the annual Opera Ball, during which audience members are allowed backstage to mingle with the stars.

2 Akademie der bildenden Künste Art Collections

📍 L6 🏛 Schillerplatz 3 🕙 10am–6pm Tue–Sun 🌐 kunstsammlungen akademie.at ↗

The Academy of Fine Arts Vienna, designed by Theophil von Hansen, occupies an elegant Italian Renaissance-style Ringstrasse building. Completed in 1876, it possesses outstanding collections of paintings, with works by Titian, Rembrandt, Rubens and Hieronymus Bosch, as well as some interesting graphic art. Reflecting its location in a modern art school, the Art Collections regularly exhibit selected masterpieces in thought-provoking combination with international contemporary art.

3 Schiller Monument

📍 L6 🏛 Schillerplatz

The main focal point of Schillerplatz, the charming square situated right in front of the Academy of Fine Arts, is the statue of the poet and dramatist Friedrich Schiller, sculpted in 1876 by Johannes Schilling. Opposite to it is the Goethe monument *(p59)*, created by Edmund von Hellmer in 1900 as a tribute to another great German-language writer.

4 Secession Building

This late-19th-century building *(p46)* is a remarkable celebration of the Secessionist artistic movement founded by famous artist Gustav Klimt in 1897. The building houses contemporary art exhibitions.

Detail from the interior of the Theater an der Wien

5 Theater an der Wien
F3 **Linke Wienzeile 6**
theater-wien.at

Emanuel Schikaneder, a friend of Mozart, founded this theatre in 1801. It remained closed for many years, until it opened its doors once again in 2006 on Mozart's 250th birth anniversary. Now billed as "The New Opera House of Vienna", it stages an opera premiere every month. There is a youthful repertory company and a programme of song and youth opera called the *Kammeroper* or "Chamber Opera". Performances of Mozart are frequent, but contemporary opera is also featured here. Backstage tours can be booked in advance.

6 Majolika Haus
F3 **Linke Wienzeile 40**

One of the finest examples of an Art Nouveau-style house was designed by the celebrated architect Otto Wagner (*p127*) in 1898. The house is deco-rated with colourful floral patterns on small glazed tiles, known as majolica – pink roses, green leaves and blue blossoms spread across the building's surface. The house is now divided into apartments with shops on the ground floor.

7 Wagner Haus
F3 **Linke Wienzeile 38**

Next to the Majolika Haus is another of Otto Wagner's Art Nouveau-style buildings. The six-storey house has a white plastered façade with golden stucco elements. Between the top row of windows are golden medallions with female heads, designed by 19th-century Austrain painter Koloman Moser. Peacock feathers trail under the medallions reaching down to the windows below. Above the rounded corner with an iron-and-glass porch are statues of female "callers" by Othmar Schimkowitz (1864–1947).

8 Naschmarkt
F4 **Between Karlsplatz and Kettenbrückengasse** **6am–7:30pm Mon–Fri, 6am–5pm Sat** **naschmarkt-vienna.com**

The city's largest market, bustling Naschmarkt is a colourful place with more than 100 stalls selling a wide variety of products. At 6am, vendors selling fruit, vegetables, flowers, meat and fish open their stalls. On Saturdays, farmers from outside the city offer their produce, and at the Saturday flea market, stalls sell everything from antiques to second-hand clothing.

9 Mariahilfer Strasse
K6

After Kärntner Strasse and the Graben, this pedestrianized street is Vienna's trendiest and busiest shopping mile.

Shops and cafés lining Mariahilfer Strasse

A MUSICAL CITY

Vienna is inextricably connected with classical music and is often referred to as the world's musical capital. The art-loving Habsburgs acted as paymasters and provided the perfect setting for a thriving musical landscape, particularly from the late 18th to the 19th centuries. Today the traditions of its past remain, but there is also a vivid scene of contemporary music in the city.

Hundreds of shops and a few department stores offer fashion, books, music and electronic goods, while cafés, restaurants, ice-cream parlours and cinemas abound.

10 Hofmobiliendepot

- F1 Andreasgasse 7
- 10am–5pm Tue–Sun
- moebelmuseumwien.at

In the Imperial Furniture Collection, established in the late 18th century by Empress Maria Theresa, all the Habsburgs' furniture was stored, repaired and kept in a good state to be distributed to imperial households when required. Today, the museum tells how imperial families used to live, and has thousands of exhibits – from the everyday to the highly unusual – spanning more than five centuries.

A DAY IN THE OPERA AND NASCHMARKT AREA

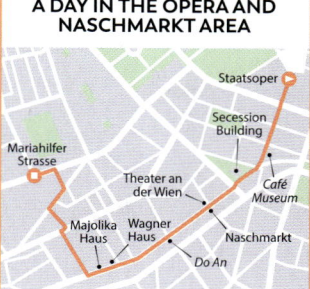

Morning

Start off by admiring the majestic, Neo-Renaissance **Staatsoper** (*p44*) and cut your way through Operngasse toward the **Secession Building** (*p46*). Observe the beautiful exterior of Olbrich's Secessionist masterpiece, with its ornate dome made up of gilt laurel leaves, and don't miss the stunning *Beethoven Frieze* inside this Art Nouveau building.

For a coffee and snack break, head to the historic **Café Museum** (*p122*), first designed by Adolf Loos in 1899.

Walk towards **Naschmarkt**, and roam the market, casting a glance over the road to the **Theater an der Wien**, the **Majolika Haus** (*see p115*) and the **Wagner Haus**.

For lunch, choose from one of the many cafés or restaurants on Naschmarkt, such as the bustling **Do An** (*p123*).

Afternoon

Make your way up to **Mariahilfer Strasse** and spend the afternoon looking around the many shops.

Stay in the area for the evening and attend a classical opera show, either in the **Theater an der Wien** or in the **Staatsoper**. But, whichever of the two venues you choose, make sure you have booked your tickets in advance.

Cafés and Bars

1. Café Drechsler
F2 **Linke Wienzeile 22**
drechsler-wien.at
Elegantly remodelled by British architects Conran and Partners, this legendary coffee house has regained its mantle as the best place for a late-night drink or an early breakfast.

2. Café Sperl
K6 **Gumpendorfer Strasse 11**
cafesperl.at
This stylish café has been in business since the 19th century and has always had a reputation for being the haunt of artists, musicians, actors and nobles.

3. Barfly's Club
F2 **Esterhazygasse 33**
barflys.at
Situated in the Hotel Fürst Metternich, this fashionable bar serves a huge selection of cocktails, whiskies and rums, which complement the regular live jazz and swing music.

4. Wein & Co Bar
L6 **Linke Wienzeile 4**
weinco.at
Right by the Secession Building (*p46*), this trendy place is a wine shop cum bar with more than 60 wines from across the globe. It also serves Italian fare.

5. Naschmarkt Deli
F4 **Naschmarkt stall 421–36**
naschmarktdeli.at
This little café set amid the bustling Naschmarkt market stalls serves excellent breakfasts all day long and offers all kinds of cuisines, from Viennese to Turkish.

6. Café Museum
M5 **Operngasse 7**
cafemuseum.at
Adolf Loos's minimalist coffee house makes for a great place to people-watch while enjoying coffee and delicious cakes.

7. Tanzcafé Jenseits
F2 **Nelhengasse 3**
tanzcafejenseits.com
An intimate little bar with plush reddish decor, which gives it a slightly faded, Hollywood-of-yesteryear feel. There is also a small dance floor.

8. Alt Wien Kaffee
F4 **Schleifmühlgasse 23**
altwien.at
Alt Wien Kaffee is a small roastery that serves a wide range of brews and coffee packs to take home.

9. Café Europa
E2 **Zollergasse 8**
cafeeuropa.at
This spot is as close as you'll come to an all-night American diner in Vienna, both in its ambience and its extensive menu. Sip on flavourful drinks and tuck into hearty food.

10. Café Ritter
F2 **Mariahilfer Strasse 73**
caferitter.at
A traditional café just off the main shopping drag, Café Ritter offers a variety of delicious coffees, cakes and snacks. It makes for a great break from nearby shopping.

Lovely dining area at Café Sperl

Outdoor seating at Do An in Naschmarkt

Places to Eat

1. Umarfisch
📍 F3 🏠 Naschmarkt Stand 76–9
🚫 Sun 🌐 umarfisch.at · €€
Try a seafood platter or the oysters with a glass of sparkling wine here.

2. Výtopna
📍 F3 🏠 Rechte Wienzeile 21/1
🚫 Mon & Tue 🌐 vytopna.at · €
At this restaurant, drinks and food are delivered to your table by a digitally controlled model railroad.

3. Do An
📍 F4 🏠 Naschmarkt stall 412 🚫 Sun
🌐 doan.at · €
Do An offers an excellent menu – the smoked tofu with sautéed courgettes, carrots and spring onions is delicious.

4. Salzberg
📍 G2 🏠 Magdalenenstrasse 17
📞 01 581 62 26 · €€
Creative Viennese dishes are paired with beer specially brewed in eastern Austria. The weekend brunch buffet here is particularly good.

5. Zu den drei Buchteln
📍 G3 🏠 Wehrgasse 9 🚫 Sun
🌐 zu-den-3-buchteln.webflow.io · €€
This friendly place serves Bohemian specialities such as yeast cakes, known as *buchteln*.

6. Steman
📍 F1 🏠 Otto-Bauer Gasse 7
🚫 Sat & Sun 🌐 steman.at · €€
Enjoy a prebooked wine tasting or dine at long tables at this cosy

PRICE CATEGORIES

For a three-course meal for one with half a bottle of wine (or equivalent meal), taxes and extra charges.

€ under €35 €€ €35–70 €€€ over €70

part-wooden-panelled place serving traditional Viennese fare.

7. Wandel
📍 E2 🏠 Stuchgasse 6
🚫 Mon & Sun 🌐 wandel.wien · €
The speciality at this restaurant just off Burggasse is *spätzle*, a type of pasta that's a staple in many parts of southern Germany and Austria.

8. Restaurant Wiener
📍 E1 🏠 Hermanngasse 27A
🌐 restaurant-wiener.at · €€
Traditional Viennese dishes are served at this old-fashioned restaurant set in a vaulted dining room.

9. Centimeter
📍 E6 🏠 Stiftgasse 4
🌐 centimeter.at · €
At Centimeter you can enjoy pub-style dining in a cosy bar-like setting. The ribs, burgers and schnitzel are popular, as are the vegan and vegetarian options.

10. Chang
📍 F4 🏠 Waaggasse 1 🚫 Sun
🌐 chang.at · €€
Simple, reasonably priced Asian food is served at this modern noodle bar. Try the weekly lunchtime set menus.

FROM KARLSKIRCHE TO THE BELVEDERE

The area from Karlskirche to the Belvedere is filled with grand mansions and summer residences from the 18th and 19th centuries. Vienna's aristocracy built their summer palaces here thanks to its countryside location not too far from the city. Prince Eugene's summer retreat, the Belvedere, dominates the area, but there are several other ornate homes, such as the Palais Schwarzenberg and the Palais Hoyos, which are well worth a visit. Today, many such buildings are embassies and some of the once-private gardens are now public parks. During Roman times, the civil settlement of the Vindobona military camp was situated here. The area's main roads, Landstrasser Hauptstrasse and Rennweg, follow old Roman routes.

Top 10 Sights p125

Places to Eat p129

Cafés and Bars p128

For places to stay in this area, see p148

1 Salesianerinnenkirche

📍 F6 🏠 Rennweg 8–10
🕐 7am Mon–Sat & 9am
Sun 🌐 salesianerinnen.at

Amalia Wilhelmina (1673–1742), the widow of Emperor Joseph I, founded this monastery of the Salesian order in 1717 in thanks for her recovery from smallpox. The architect Donato Felice d'Allio completed the complex with its eight large courtyards in 1728. Along with the historic Belvedere and Palais Schwarzenberg, it forms a magnificent Baroque ensemble. The dome is decorated with frescoes by the Rococo painter Giovanni Antonio Pellegrini (1675–1741) showing the Virgin Mary's ascension to heaven. In accordance with Amalia Wilhelmina's will, her body is buried under the high altar, but an urn with her heart was placed inside her husband's coffin in the imperial crypt on Neuer Markt.

2 Musikverein

📍 N6 🏠 Musikvereinsplatzl
🌐 musikverein.at 🔗

This impressive concert hall in the Greek Renaissance style was built by Theophil von Hansen in 1869 for the Society of Friends of Music. It became famous after the Vienna Philharmonic Orchestra began giving their annual New Year's Concert here in 1941. There

Orchestra performing at the Golden Hall, Musikverein

are three performance areas, but the main auditorium, the Golden Hall, is the finest, with lavish decorations and great acoustics. It is advisable to book a guided tour via the website ahead of your visit.

3 The Belvedere

These two 18th-century palace buildings (*p36*) are linked by landscaped gardens, featuring tiered fountains and cascades, with statues of nymphs.

4 Karlskirche

This Baroque masterpiece (*p40*) is one of Vienna's most impressive churches, with its beautiful carved columns and green dome.

Impressive Baroque exterior of the Karlskirche

5 Gardekirche

📍 F5 🏠 Rennweg 5a

The construction of this Rococo church was decreed by Empress Maria Theresa in 1755, and her favourite architect Nikolaus von Pacassi (1716–90) completed the building in 1763. The plain, cubic structure with a red tiled roof and a green cupola was the church to the nearby military hospital. The interior is decorated with elaborate stucco work, and behind the high altar is the painting *Christ on the Crucifix* by Peter Strudel, the founder of Vienna's first art school. The church has been the Polish national church in Vienna since 1897.

6 Liberation Monument

📍 F5 🏠 Schwarzenbergplatz

This monument to the Soviet Red Army is a reminder of Vienna's postwar history, when the city was occupied by the four Allied powers and divided into four zones. Schwarzenbergplatz was part of the Soviet zone and renamed Stalinplatz. The long marble colonnade, installed in 1845, features a statue of an armed soldier on the top. At the end of Allied occupation in 1955, the republic pledged to keep and maintain the monument.

7 Schwarzenberggarten

📍 F5 🏠 Schwarzenbergplatz 9
🚫 To the public

In 1697, the noted Baroque architect Lukas von Hildebrandt was commissioned to build a summer palace here, which was purchased by the influential Schwarzenberg family in 1720. Architects Johann Fischer von Erlach and his son Josef Emanuel continued adorning the palace and laid out the garden in formal French style.

8 Otto Wagner Pavilion

📍 F4 🏠 Karlsplatz 🕐 Mid-Mar–Oct: 10am–1pm & 2–5pm Fri–Sun
🚫 Public hols 🌐 wienmuseum.at/otto_wagner_pavillon_karlsplatz 🔗

The two pavilions on Karlsplatz were built by renowned architect Otto Wagner in 1897 as twin stations for the Vienna City Train, the horse-drawn and later steam-powered predecessors of today's underground rail system. In total, Wagner designed 34 stations and various bridges and viaducts for the train line that was finished in 1901. The pavilions on Karlsplatz are made of steel and marble slabs, and the roof over the arched gate is decorated with golden ornaments. Both stations

OTTO WAGNER

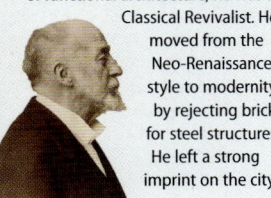

Before Otto Wagner (1841–1918) became one of Vienna's most eminent architects and an advocate of functional architecture, he was a Classical Revivalist. He moved from the Neo-Renaissance style to modernity by rejecting brick for steel structures. He left a strong imprint on the city.

became obsolete once the modern underground lines had been built. Today the Otto Wagner Pavilion is used by the Wien Museum and the other station is a café.

9 Theresianum
🗺 G4 🚇 Favoritenstrasse 15
🚫 To the public

On the site of this elite private school once stood an imperial summer palace, until it was destroyed by Turkish troops in 1683. On its ruins the Italian architect Lodovico Burnacini built the Theresianum (1687–90). Comprising a long building with a sober façade, it was named after Empress Maria Theresa, who installed an educational institute here in 1746 for the young nobility. Today it is a top private school and a diplomatic academy.

10 Palais Hoyos
🗺 F5 🚇 Rennweg 3
🚫 To the public

Otto Wagner built this Neo-Renaissance palace as his home in 1891, before he joined the Vienna Secessionist movement. The palace was later bought by Countess Marie Hoyos. The windows of the upper floor are framed with intricate floral details, but the ground and first floors are built in sombre pale stone.

Otto Wagner Pavilion at Karlsplatz

A DAY'S WALK FROM KARLSPLATZ TO THE BELVEDERE

Morning

Start your day at **Karlsplatz** to inspect the **Otto Wagner Pavilion** in Resselpark and then walk on to the splendid **Karlskirche** (*p40*). Left of the church is the **Wien Museum Karlsplatz** (*p60*), a great place to study the city's history. Don't miss the Klimt and Schiele paintings, as well as Adolf Loos's original living room from 1903.

Head towards **Argentinierstrasse** where you can enjoy some coffee and cake in **Café Goldegg** (*p128*).

Walk east to the **Liberation Monument**, then take Rennweg and pass by **Palais Hoyos**. For lunch, pop into **Salm Bräu** (*p128*).

Afternoon

Head for the Belvedere (*p36*), where you can easily spend the rest of the day. After having a look around the exhibition in the **Lower Belvedere**, walk through the formal gardens towards the **Upper Belvedere**, home to the Austrian National Gallery with many Klimt, Schiele, Gerstl and Attersee paintings. You can also visit the nearby **Belvedere 21 gallery** (*p37*), located on Arsenalstrasse 1. It holds changing exhibitions of Austrian art from 1945 to the present day.

Enjoy a classical music concert in the **Musikverein** (*p125*), but be sure to book a day in advance.

Cafés and Bars

Rustic interior with wooden furnishings at Salm Bräu

in the former residence of the Prince of Württemberg. Enjoy a cup of coffee paired with the café's signature tortes.

5. Bristol Lounge
📍 E4 🏠 Mahlerstrasse 5
🌐 dastriest.at

Expect live piano music, an open fireplace and one of the finest wine lists in Vienna. Proximity to the State Opera House *(p44)* draws a formal crowd.

6. Café Wortner
📍 G4 🏠 Wiedner Hauptstrasse 55
🌐 wortner.at

A historic coffee house with a whiff of the Biedermeier era about it. Its outdoor seating area is particularly charming.

1. Salm Bräu
📍 F5 🏠 Rennweg 8 🌐 salmbraeu.com

Hearty dishes are complemented by beers brewed in-house at Salm Bräu. Try the different sausage specialities and bread with various options.

7. Café Karl-Otto
📍 F4 🏠 Otto Wagner Pavilion, Karlsplatz 🌐 jugendstil-cafe.at

Karl-Otto is a popular café-restaurant serving traditional Viennese food by day, and a club with international DJs spinning lively tracks by night.

2. Café Schwarzenberg
📍 N6 🏠 Kärntner Ring 17
🌐 cafe-schwarzenberg.at

A traditional café with plush interiors, Schwarzenberg offers outdoor seating on its terrace in the summer. It also hosts jazz breakfasts and changing exhibitions of Viennese artists. Thursday through Sunday, evenings come alive with fantastic piano concerts.

8. Flanagan's Irish Pub
📍 N5 🏠 Schwarzenbergstrasse 1–3
🌐 lanagans.at

Enjoy a few pints of Guinness in a traditional Irish pub setting. The furniture was imported from Cork.

3. Café Goldegg
📍 H5 🏠 Argentinierstrasse 49, corner of Goldeggasse 🌐 cafe goldegg.at

A peaceful café and a retreat for reading, Goldegg also has a games room where you can play chess or cards.

9. Point of Sale
📍 F4 🏠 Schleifmühlgasse 12
🌐 thepointofsale.at

This modern designer café serves international breakfasts, snacks and tarts until late into the afternoon.

4. Café Imperial
📍 N6 🏠 Kärntner Ring 16
🌐 cafe-imperial.at

This historic café opened in 1873 for the Universal Exhibition and is based

10. Artner auf der Wieden
📍 G4 🏠 Floragasse 6
🌐 artner.co.at

A cosy wine bar and restaurant. Try the homemade goat's cheese marinated in olive oil and herbs. You can also take a bottle home with you from the wine boutique.

Places to Eat

1. EssDur
🄿 P6 🄰 Am Heumarkt 6
🅦 essdur.at · €€
Enjoy a pre-concert evening meal at EssDur, the in-house restaurant of the magnificent Konzerthaus.

2. Santa Lucia
🄿 F6 🄰 Salesianergasse 10 🅦 pizzeria-ristorante-santa-lucia.at · €
Vienna's only Italian-Indian restaurant is a favourite with locals. There's free tiramisu with every dinner.

3. Wieden Bräu
🄿 G4 🄰 Waaggasse 5
🅦 wieden-braeu.at · €
This beerhall and beer garden serves Viennese food and has a brewery that offers tours and makes its own beer.

4. Art Corner
🄿 G5 🄰 Prinz-Eugen-Straße 56/1
🅦 artcorner.restaurant · €€
Located close to the Belvedere, Art Corner serves Austrian and Mediterranean delicacies with alfresco dining. The owner will give you a warm welcome.

5. Ribs of Vienna
🄿 N4 🄰 Weihburggasse 22
🅦 ribsofvienna.at · €€
Set in a 16th-century vaulted basement, the characterful ambience of this restaurant will transport you back in time. The bench tables are perfect for large groups. Don't miss the "one-metre spare ribs".

6. Gasthaus Ubl
🄿 F3 🄰 Pressgasse 26
🄲 01 587 64 37 🕒 Mon & Tue · €
Probably Vienna's last simply styled *gasthaus*, this is the perfect place for dinner. Classic Viennese food is served in oak-panelled surroundings.

PRICE CATEGORIES
For a three-course meal for one with half a bottle of wine (or equivalent meal), taxes and extra charges.

€ under €35 €€ €35–70 €€€ over €70

7. Wiener Wiazhaus
🄿 F4 🄰 Karlsgasse 22
🅦 wiener-wiazhaus.com · €
The perfect lunch spot, this retro pub-restaurant serves home-style dishes in a casual setting.

8. Gmoa Keller
🄿 P6 🄰 Am Heumarkt 25 🕒 Sun & public hols 🅦 gmoakeller.at · €€
Favoured by musicians from the concert halls nearby, this place is known for its schnitzels, seasonal dishes and wines.

9. Wiener Wirtschaft
🄿 G4 🄰 Wiedner Hauptstrasse 27–9
🅦 wienerwirtschaft.com · €€
A short walk away from Karlsplatz, this restaurant serves Austrian dishes and its speciality, gulash.

10. Fine Fine all'Italiana
🄿 G5 🄰 Argentinierstrasse 15
🅦 finefine.at · €€
This lovely Italian restaurant has a modern dining room and serves delectable Mediterranean cuisine.

Traditional Viennese cuisine at Wieden Bräu beerhall

GREATER VIENNA

The city of Vienna is located where the splendid hills of the Vienna Woods slope down into the Wiener Becken (the Vienna basin); from here the city spreads out on both sides of the Danube. The woods provide a welcome green belt and a recreation area for city dwellers. Today's suburbs, such as Grinzing and Nussdorf, were once countryside villages, until the city swallowed them up. In the 17th and 18th centuries the city's noble families built their summer residences within easy reach of the capital, but far enough out to benefit from cool rural surroundings during the hottest time of the year. Schloss Schönbrunn, Geymüllerschlössel and Hermesvilla were such examples. Also away from the busy urban centre, for reasons of hygiene and space, is the country's largest cemetery, the Zentralfriedhof.

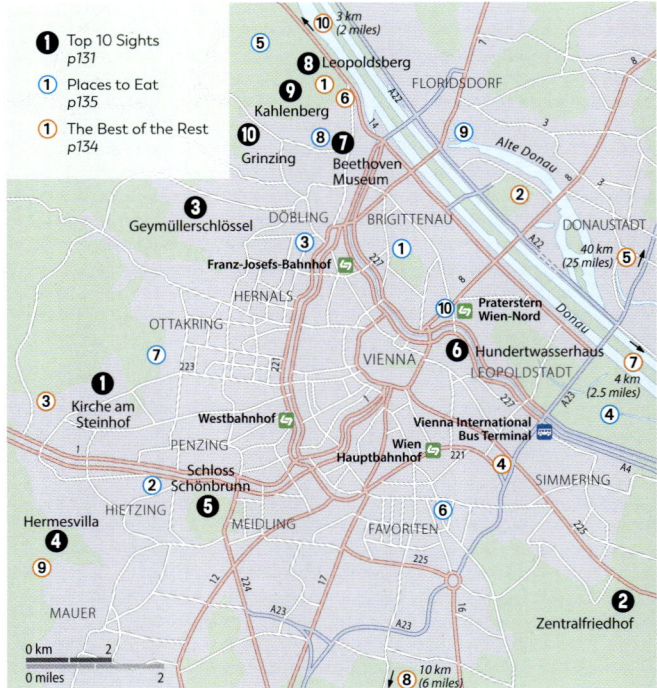

1 Top 10 Sights *p131*

1 Places to Eat *p135*

1 The Best of the Rest *p134*

For places to stay in this area, see p149

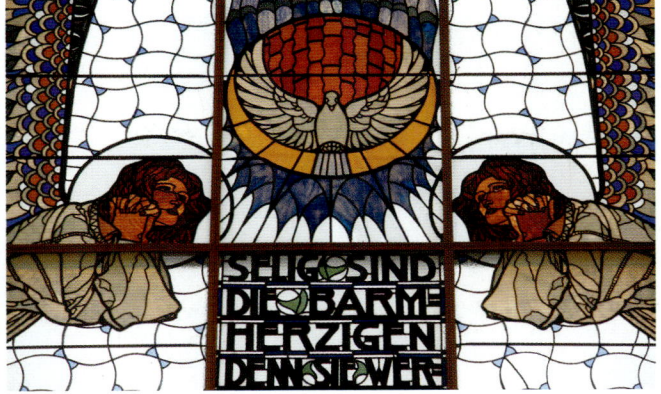

Beautiful stained glass at Kirche am Steinhof

1 Kirche am Steinhof

🏠 Baumgartner Höhe 1
🕐 4–5pm Sat, noon–4pm Sun
🌐 wienmuseum.at/otto_wagner_kirche_am_steinhof 🚻♿

Another one of Otto Wagner's *(p127)* masterpieces, this church was built between 1905 and 1907 as a place of worship for the patients at the Steinhof psychiatric hospital. The hospital complex at the edge of the Vienna Woods was designed to bring patients closer to a healthy and natural environment to help with their recovery. The church's golden dome can be seen from the Gloriette building in Schönbrunn Park.

2 Zentralfriedhof

🏠 Simmeringer Hauptstrasse
🕐 Dawn–dusk daily

More than three million people have been buried in this 2.5-ha (6-acre) cemetery since it opened in 1874, among them 500 Austrian politicians, composers and actors. Max Hegele, Otto Wagner's student, designed the entrance portal, the mortuary and the Dr-Karl-Lueger-Gedächtniskirche, named after a Vienna mayor (1897–1910). The church is among Vienna's most important Art Nouveau buildings. Within the Zentralfriedhof are separate burial areas for followers of different faiths. There's also a beautiful park where visitors can relax.

3 Geymüllerschlössel

🏠 Pötzleinsdorferstrasse 102
📞 711 36 298 🕐 10am–6pm Sat & Sun 🚻
The Geymüllerschlössel is a summer palace reflecting the Biedermeier style. Owned by the Museum of Applied Arts, it houses 170 clocks, among them an early Viennese flute clock (c 1800) that plays music by the Austrian composer Joseph Haydn *(p66)*.

4 Hermesvilla

🏠 Lainzer Tiergarten 🕐 Mid-Mar–Oct: 10am–6pm Tue–Sun & public hols 🌐 wienmuseum.at/hermesvilla_en 🚻

Emperor Franz Joseph had this palace built for his wife Elisabeth between 1882 and 1886 by architect Karl von Hasenauer. The Hermes statue in the park gives it the name. The fine palace interior features murals by Gustav Klimt, Franz Matsch and Hugo Charlemont.

5 Schloss Schönbrunn

This imperial Baroque palace *(p50)*, with its stunning landscaped gardens, is one of Vienna's most visited sights. Built in the late 16th century by Maximilian II, the structure originally served as a hunting lodge and was named for a spring that flowed in the vicinity.

Multicoloured exterior of the Hundertwasserhaus

6 Hundertwasserhaus
With perhaps the most unusual and colourful private residences in the world, this apartment block *(p48)* was built in 1985 by artist Friedensreich Hundertwasser.

7 Beethoven Museum
🏠 Probusgasse 6 🕐 10am–1pm & 2–6pm Tue–Sun 🖥 wienmuseum.at/beethoven_museum 🔗

German composer and pianist Ludwig van Beethoven spent his summers in this small house. In 2017, the building was expanded by the Wien Museum and inaugurated as the first full-scale Beethoven Museum in Vienna. The famous composer came to the then-rural village of Heligenstäder for its healing mineral springs to gain relief

Lush vineyards in the village of Grinzing

for his deafness. Unfortunately, nothing helped. In 1802, while he was still here, he wrote the "Heiligenstädter Testament", a poignant letter to his brothers. The letter was, however, never sent.

8 Leopoldsberg
Dominating the Danube valley is the Leopoldsberg mountain. From its peak at 425 m (1,400 ft), you get an excellent view of the entire region around Vienna. Leopoldsberg is named after the Babenberg ruler Leopold III (1073–1136) and the ruins of the 13th-century Babenberg castle destroyed by the Turks in 1529 are still visible. An older church on top of the mountain was also destroyed by the Turks and was replaced by a Baroque church in the 18th century. Next to Leopoldsberg is its slightly higher twin peak, Kahlenberg.

9 Kahlenberg
Covered with lush trees and vineyards, the 484-m- (1,580-ft-) high Kahlenberg mountain is on the edge of the Vienna Woods. The Höhenstrasse, a scenic route lined with trees, occasionally offers a glimpse of the city. It winds its way up from Grinzing, and its peak offers a breathtaking view of Vienna. During the Turkish siege of 1683, the Polish troops under King Jan III Sobieski

VIENNA WOODS

The Vienna Woods spread towards the west of the city and were turned into a protected area as early as 1467 by Emperor Frederick III. Industrialization in the 19th century threatened large swathes of this forestland, but public resistance preserved the area's protected status in the late 20th century. Today, the Vienna Woods are as popular for excursions as ever.

descended from the top of this hill to defeat the Turkish army on 12 September that year. The little Baroque church on top of Kahlenberg commemorates this historic event.

10 Grinzing

Vienna is the only capital in the world where wine grapes are grown within the city boundaries – some 675 ha (1,670 acres) of vineyards are found here. The most widely known wine-growing community in the city is Grinzing. Once a small vintners' village on the outskirts of the city, Grinzing still has many narrow streets that retain an old-fashioned rural charm. The village is divided into the Oberer Ort and Unterer Ort (upper and lower towns). Today, it is a hub of *heurigen (p82)*, with crowds of both locals and tourists flocking to the wine taverns.

A DAY IN VIENNA'S OUTSKIRTS

Morning

Begin your day at the former imperial summer residence **Schloss Schönbrunn** *(p50)*. Spend some time in the palace, walking in the park and the formal French garden, or visiting the world's oldest zoo at Schönbrunn Park. For a relaxing drink and great views, head to the far end of the park to the coffee house in the Gloriette building.

Stroll through the park towards the Hietzinger gate of the palace. Just around the corner is the Plachutta Heitzing *(plachutta.at)*, where you can try *tafelspitz (p79)* for lunch.

Afternoon

After lunch, head to the **Kirche am Steinhof** *(p131)*. Take the U4 Schönbrunn U-bahn to the Unter St Veit stop, then cross the street to reach the 47A bus stop. Take the bus from here. It will pass Baumgarten cemetery en route to the Otto Wagner Hospital. From here a path winds up to the church.

From the Kirche am Steinhof opt to head to the leafy *heurigen* of **Grinzing** for a relaxing evening.

Walk north from the church on the footpath to **Pönningerweg**. From here the 46A bus takes you to **Ottakring station**. Next, take the S45 Schnellbahn train to **Wien Oberdöbling Bahnhof**, from where the 38 tram goes straight to **Grinzing**.

Boating in the Kühwörter Wasser lake, Lobau National Park

The Best of the Rest

1. Nussdorf
Nussdorf's picturesque location amid hills overgrown with vineyards is complemented by its long narrow streets.

2. Vienna International Centre
🏛 Wagramerstrasse 5 🕐 For tours: 9am–5pm Mon–Fri 🌐 unvienna.org
🚇🚃
Also known as the UNO City, this is the Vienna headquarters of the UN. Adjacent to the complex lies the Donaupark and its iconic Donauturm (Danube Tower; *donauturm.at*).

3. Ernst Fuchs Museum
🏛 Hüttelbergstrasse 26 🕐 10am–4pm Tue–Sun 🌐 ernstfuchs museum.at 🚇
Housed in a stunning villa with pastel-coloured walls and ornate portals, the Ernst Fuchs Museum was built by Otto Wagner *(p127)* and later altered by Austrian painter Ernst Fuchs. The latter's artworks are on display here.

4. Sankt-Marxer-Friedhof
🏛 Leberstrasse 6–8 🕐 6:30am–6:30pm daily (Apr–Sep: to 8pm)
The final resting place of prominent Austrians, including Mozart.

5. Schloss Hof
🏛 Imperial Festival Palace Hof 🕐 Hours vary, check website 🌐 schlosshof.at
This was the former country seat of Prince Eugene of Savoy and later Empress Maria Theresa.

6. Lehár-Schikaneder Schlössl
🏛 Hachhofergasse 18 📞 01 318 5416
This Baroque palace was once home to Emanuel Schikaneder, who wrote the libretto for *The Magic Flute*, and later to composer Franz Lehár. Call ahead to book an appointment.

7. Lobau National Park
The Lobau is wild national parkland, locally known as "Vienna's jungle". It features pretty lakes, secluded forests and wildlife.

8. Laxenburg
The main attraction in this pretty town is the 18th-century Laxenburg Palace *(schloss-laxenberg.at)* and its lovely park.

9. Lainzer Tiergarten
🏛 1130 Vienna 🕐 8am–dush daily 🌐 lainzer-tiergarten.at
Once a Habsburg hunting ground, this is now a wildlife refuge home to wild boar, deer and bighorn sheep, with several sheltered observation areas and walkways. From the entrance, a 15-minute walk through woods and meadows brings you to the Hermesvilla *(p131)*, a favourite summer retreat of the imperial family.

10. Klosterneuburg
This ancient town has an impressive Augustine abbey *(stift-klosterneuburg. at)*, which was founded in the early 12th century by Babenberg ruler Leopold III. If visiting in July, don't miss the opera festival *(p90)* that takes place in the abbey's courtyard.

Places to Eat

1. Mraz and Sohn
🏠 Wallensteinstrasse 59
🕐 Sat, Sun & public hols
🌐 mrazundsohn.at · €€€

The two-Michelin-starred Mraz and Sohn is one of the best restaurants in Vienna. The chefs' innovative cooking can be enjoyed in a relaxed setting.

2. Café Dommayer-Oberlaa
🏠 Corner Dommayergasse, Auhofstrasse 2 🌐 oberlaa-wien.at · €

Dommayer-Oberlaa is a traditional café with red velvet upholstery, a wooden veranda and a pretty garden. Johann Strauss (p67) used to perform here.

3. Fischer Bräu
🏠 Billrothstrasse 17 🌐 fischer braeu.at · €

There is a pleasant beer garden at this restaurant and pub, which has wooden interiors and its own brewery.

4. Café-Restaurant Lusthaus
🏠 Freudenau 254, end of Prater Hauptallee 🕐 Oct–Apr: Wed & Thu 🌐 lusthaus-wien.at · €€

This octagonal pavilion in Prater park was built in 1874 as a meeting point for the imperial hunting party. Lusthaus is now a charming restaurant with lovely views of the park.

5. Skyline Lounge Restaurant
🏠 Am Kahlenberg 2–3
🌐 kahlenberg.wien · €€€

Perfect for a special occasion, the Skyline Lounge Restaurant offers a multi-course menu that can be enjoyed on the terrace along with panoramic views of Vienna.

6. Meixner's Gastwirtschaft
🏠 Buchengasse 64 🕐 Sat & Sun
🌐 meixners-gastwirtschaft.at · €€

Family-owned restaurant Meixner's Gastwirtschaft prepares Viennese cuisine at the highest level. Be sure to sample the Austrian lamb.

PRICE CATEGORIES

For a three-course meal for one with half a bottle of wine (or equivalent meal), taxes and extra charges.

€ under €35 €€ €35–70 €€€ over €70

7. Plachuttas Grünspan
🏠 Ottakringer Strasse 266
🌐 plachutta-gruenspan.at · €€

Vienna's most acclaimed beer garden, Plachuttas Grünspan has indoor seating all year round.

8. Amador
🏠 Grinzingerstrasse 86 🕐 Sat–Tue
🌐 restaurant-amador.com · €€€

Set within a vaulted cellar, Amador is a three-Michelin-starred restaurant that offers daring gastronomy and superb wine.

9. La Creperie
🏠 An der Oberen Alten Donau 6
📞 01 270 31 00 · €€

Open until midnight, this creperie is frequented by tourists and locals alike.

10. Edlingers-Tempel
🗺 B6 🏠 Praterstrasse 56 🕐 Mon & public hols 🌐 geschmacks-tempel.at · €€

Located near the house where The Blue Danube waltz was penned, Edlingers-Tempel offers inexpensive set lunch menus in an intimate setting.

Alfresco dining at Meixner's Gastwirtschaft

STREETSMART

A tram outside the Vienna State Opera

GETTING AROUND

Whether you're exploring Vienna by foot or making use of public transport, here is everything you need to navigate the city and the areas beyond the centre like a pro.

AT A GLANCE

PUBLIC TRANSPORT COSTS
These tickets are valid on all means of public transport (U-Bahn, tram, bus and night bus) in Vienna.

CITY CENTRE SINGLE

€2.40

Single journey
within one zone

24-HOUR PASS

€8

Unlimited travel
within Vienna

48-HOUR PASS

€14.10

Unlimited travel
within Vienna

SPEED LIMITS

MOTORWAY

130 km/h
(80mph)

REGIONAL ROAD

100 km/h
(60mph)

URBAN AREA

50 km/h
(30mph)

RESIDENTIAL AREA

30 km/h
(20mph)

Arriving by Air

Found 19 km (12 miles) southeast of the city centre, **Vienna International Airport**, known locally as Schwechat, serves over 100 airlines.

Taxis will take passengers to the centre for a fixed €25. Buses from Vienna Airport Lines go to all major areas for €8 (under 14s free). A non-stop City Airport Train called **CAT** offers luxury seating and a 16-minute ride to Wien Mitte train station for €14.90 (under 12s free). The OBB Railjet high-speed train takes 15 minutes and costs €4.50, stopping at the Hauptbahnhof railway station. There's also the S7, a slightly slower train that stops at the more centrally located Wien Mitte and Wien Praterstern stations. It takes 25 and 30 minutes, respectively, and is the same price as the Railjet.
CAT
w cityairporttrain.com
Vienna International Airport
w viennaairport.com

Bus Travel

Vienna's main coach station, the **Vienna International Bus Terminal** (VIB), is located close to Erdberg U3 underground station. Services arrive here from most major European cities.

Postbus and **Flixbus** run routes throughout Austria and Slovakia. Coaches arrive in Vienna at the Wien Hauptbahnhof bus terminal.
Flixbus
w flixbus.co.uk
Postbus
w postbus.at
Vienna International Bus Terminal
w vib-wien.at

Train Travel

Austria has an efficient high-speed rail network and reliable local services, the vast majority of which are run by **Österreichische Bundesbahnen** (Austrian Federal Railways), more commonly known as ÖBB.

The fastest train, the Railjet, can travel at speeds of up to 230 km/h (143 mph) and links the major Austrian cities, as well as cities across Germany, Italy, Hungary, the Czech Republic and Switzerland. Slower regional trains serve smaller towns.
Österreichische Bundesbahnen
🅦 oebb.at

Public Transport
Wiener Linien is Vienna's main public transport authority. Timetables, ticket information, transport maps and more can be obtained from Wiener Linien information and ticket offices or the Wiener Linien website. The public transport network is made up of trams (Strassenbahn), buses (Autobus) and underground trains (U-Bahn).

The city's transport system works largely thanks to an honesty system – there are no ticket barriers at stations. However, checks by transport authority staff do take place – you'll occasionally be asked for your *Fahrschein* (ticket) by a transport guard. Travellers caught without a valid ticket will be fined €103.

Rush hour on weekdays is from about 7am to 9:30am, then again from 4:30pm to 6:30pm. Smoking is banned in stations and on public transport.
Wiener Linien
🅦 wienerlinien.at

Tickets
Vienna's public transport ticketing system is less confusing than it appears at first glance. The easiest way to buy tickets is by downloading the WienMobil app on your smartphone though they are still available from counters at some U-Bahn and S-Bahn stations and from some shops.

A standard ticket covers all areas of the city and allows passengers to change trains and lines and to switch from the underground to a tram or a bus, as long as they take the most direct route and they don't break their journey.

Wiener Linien's **EASY CityPass** is a good-value option for anyone who is planning on using public transport for more than one day. The pass is available for 24, 48 and 72 hours, or a week, and also entitles the bearer to discounts at some of the city's museums, galleries and shops.

Children under 6 may travel for free on the city's transport network, while those aged between 6 and 14 qualify for half-price single tickets. The latter can also travel free during holidays, providing they can show proof of age.
EASY CityPass
🅦 easycitypass.com

U-Bahn
Vienna's underground system (U-Bahn) is a modern, clean, fast and reliable way of crossing the city. The U-Bahn's five colour-coded lines run seven days a week from around 5am to 12:30am. A 24-hour service runs on weekends and public holidays. Outside these hours, the U-Bahn service is replaced by Vienna NightLine buses. A sixth line, U5, is due to open some time between 2026 and 2032. Note that doors are opened manually and can be heavy.

Bikes are allowed on some carriages, although not before 9am or between 3pm and 6:30pm Monday to Friday.

GETTING TO AND FROM SCHWECHAT AIRPORT

Transport	Journey Time	Fare
City Airport Train (CAT)	16 mins	€14.90
S-Bahn	25 mins	€4.20
ÖBB Railjet	15 mins	€4.20
Bus	20–40 mins	€9.50
Taxi	16 mins	€25

Tram

Vienna's tram network is one of the largest in the world, with almost 30 routes. Known locally as "Bim" for its distinctive bell sound, it is a delightful way to get around the city. For the ultimate experience, seek out one of the old, traditional models with their wooden seats and vintage interiors.

Most of the main sights in Vienna's historic centre are located on the popular Ring Tram route. Passengers will need to purchase a Round-the-Ring ticket (€9) for a complete unbroken journey. Ring trams depart every 30 minutes, from 10am to 5:30pm.

Bus

Bus stops are marked with a green "H" for *Haltestelle*, or stop. Buses should stop automatically at all bus stops but if in doubt, flag it down.

Tickets purchased from the driver will be valid for one bus journey only. If you have already purchased a paper ticket from a newsagent or ticket machine, you will need to validate it in the ticket-stamping machine on the bus. If you have already made part of your journey by tram or by U-Bahn, there is no need to stamp your ticket again. Alternatively, use the WienMobil app to simplify things.

After midnight, Vienna's night bus service (marked by an "N") takes over. These operate at 30-minute intervals until 4am, starting at Schwedenplatz, the Opera and Schottentor, and together serve most suburbs.

Taxi

Taxis are a comfortable, if more expensive, way of getting around. There is a €3.80 minimum fee during the day, then €0.95 per kilometre. At night, on Sundays and on public holidays, the minimum charge is €4.30. Round the fare up to the nearest euro or 5 euros.

The "TAXI" sign on the roof will be illuminated if the vehicle is available to hail. Phone to book, or hail at a taxi stand – for Vienna-wide locations see the Vienna Taxis section on the **City of Vienna** website or download a free Vienna taxi app. Uber, which also operates in the city, has become an increasingly common way of getting around.
City of Vienna
w wien.gv.att

Driving to Austria

With the exception of Switzerland, all of Austria's neighbours are EU members, meaning there are only ad-hoc and occasional border checks.

Driving licences issued by any of the European Union member states are valid throughout the EU. If visiting from outside the EU, you may need to apply for an International Driving Permit. Check with your local automobile association before you travel.

Driving in Austria

Austria is a fairly straightforward place to drive. Roads are uniformly good and Viennese drivers generally sensible. Motorways and regional roads are easy to navigate.

Car Rental

Car-hire firms such as **Hertz** and **Sixt Rent-a-Car** can be found at Schwechat Airport. Drivers need to produce their passport, driving licence and a credit or debit card with capacity to cover the excess. Most rental agencies require drivers to be over the age of 21 and to have an international licence.
Hertz
w hertz.com
Sixt Rent-a-Car
w sixt.com

Parking

Apart from on Sundays, when shops are closed, finding a parking spot in the busy city centre of Vienna can be time consuming. The City of Vienna operates a park-and-pay scheme for all 23 districts from 9am to 10pm during the week. Parking disks are sold at newsagents (Tabak Trafiken) and petrol stations. Usually, a maximum stay of two hours is allowed in any space. In some districts, a blue line by the kerb indicates a pay-and-display scheme. Prices for car parks can vary from €5 per hour to €40 per day.

Rules of the Road
Priority is always given to the right unless a yellow diamond indicates otherwise. Unlike in other EU countries, Austrian stop lights blink rapidly in green before switching to amber. Trams, buses, police cars, fire engines and ambulances all have right of way. Vienna's speed limit is usually 50 km/h (30 mph); a limit of 30 km/h (20 mph) is enforced in residential areas.

Seatbelts are compulsory and children under the age of 12 must sit in the back, with babies and toddlers in child seats. In the event of an accident, or if a traffic jam necessitates an abrupt stop, drivers should turn on their hazard lights to warn drivers behind.

The alcohol limit is 0.5 mg per ml of blood (about 330 ml or half a pint of beer or 1–2 glasses of wine) and is strictly enforced. Spot checks are common and anyone over the limit is likely to face a fine and loss of licence.

Always carry your driving licence as well as car ownership and insurance documents. Cars on motorways and expressways are required to display a vignette toll sticker, available from all petrol stations, or to purchase a digital vignette online. Both types are valid for 1 day, 10 days, 2 months or 1 year.

Cycling
Vienna is a great city for cyclists, as long as the main roads and tramlines are avoided. A 7-km (4- mile) cycle path round the Ringstrasse takes you past many historic sights, and there are also paths to the Prater and the Hundertwasserhaus.

Keen cyclists should look out for Radkarte Wien, a booklet illustrating all of Vienna's cycle routes. Bicycles can be rented at some train stations (discounts are given with a train ticket), or from any of the 100 or so **WienMobil Bike** stations located around the city.

Cycling enthusiasts can book tours through **Pedal Power** and **Vienna Explorer**, which offers seats for children as well as e-bikes.

Pedal Power
W pedalpower.at
Vienna Explorer
W viennaexplorer.com
WienMobil Bike
W wienerlinien.at

Bicycle Safety
Ride on the right. Beware of tram tracks; cross them at an angle to avoid getting stuck. For your own safety, do not walk with your bike in a bike lane or cycle on pavements, on the side of the road, in pedestrian zones or in the dark without lights. Locals may not bother and it isn't compulsory, but wearing a helmet is recommended.

Fiaker
Once the most common form of transport in Vienna, traditional horse-drawn open carriages or Fiakers, can still be hired today at Heldenplatz, Stephansplatz and Albertinaplatz. There are several companies offering the service, which is now mainly used for special occasions.

Walking
Many of Vienna's major sites are within walking distance of each other, making it an ideal city to cover on foot. The historic Ringstrasse is perfect for a stroll: this pretty boulevard is lined with some of the city's most beautiful buildings, including the Burgtheater.

Those looking for a longer walk can travel just beyond the centre to the beautiful Vienna Woods. Here, you'll find an abundance of scenic hiking paths weaving through vineyards and passing by many picturesque towns and villages.

PRACTICAL INFORMATION

A little local know-how goes a long way in Vienna. On these pages you can find all the essential advice and information you will need to make the most of your trip to this city.

AT A GLANCE

CURRENCY
Euro (EUR)

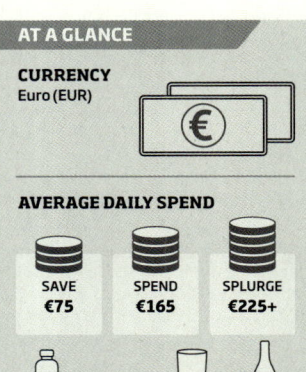

AVERAGE DAILY SPEND

SAVE	SPEND	SPLURGE
€75	**€165**	**€225+**

BOTTLED WATER	COFFEE	BEER	DINNER FOR TWO
€1.50	**€3**	**€4.50**	**€80**

ESSENTIAL PHRASES

Hello	Guten Tag
Goodbye	Auf Wiedersehen
Please	Bitte
Thank you	Danke
Do you speak English?	Sprechen Sie Englisch?
I don't understand...	Ich verstehe nicht

ELECTRICITY SUPPLY

Power sockets are type F, fitting type C and type F plugs. Standard voltage is 230 volts.

Passports and Visas

For entry requirements, including visas, consult your nearest Austrian embassy or check **Austria Info**. Citizens of the UK, US, Canada, Australia and New Zealand do not need a visa for stays of up to three months but in future must apply in advance for the European Travel Information and Authorization System (**ETIAS**). Visitors from other countries should check before travelling. EU nationals do not need a visa or an ETIAS.

Austria Info
Ⓦ austria.info
ETIAS
Ⓦ etiasvisa.com

Government Advice

Now more than ever, it is important to consult both your and the Austrian governments' advice before travelling. The UK Foreign, Commonwealth & Development Office (**FCDO**), the **US State Department**, the **Australian Department of Foreign Affairs and Trade** and the **Austrian Foreign Ministry** offer the latest on security, health and local regulations.

Australian Department of Foreign Affairs and Trade
Ⓦ smartraveller.gov.au
Austrian Foreign Ministry
Ⓦ bmeia.gv.at
UK FCDO
Ⓦ gov.uk/foreign-travel-advice
US State Department
Ⓦ travel.state.gov

Customs Information

You can find information on the laws relating to goods and currency taken in or out of Austria on the **Austrian Ministry of Finance** website.

Austrian Ministry of Finance
Ⓦ bmf.gv.at

Insurance

We recommend that you take out a comprehensive insurance policy covering theft, loss of belongings, medical care, cancellations and delays, and read the small print carefully. If your plans include sporting activities, like skiing, make sure the policy covers this.

Vaccinations

No inoculations are required to visit Austria.

Health

Emergency medical care is free for all UK and EU citizens, providing they have either a valid EHIC (European Health Insurance Card) or **GHIC** (UK Global Health Insurance Card). For other visitors, payment of hospital and other medical expenses is the patient's responsibility, so arrange comprehensive medical insurance before travelling.

To locate one of Vienna's many pharmacies (Apotheke), look out for a bright red "A" sign; there is generally one on every major street. Pharmacies run a night and Sunday rota system.

In the event of more serious illnesses and injuries, call the emergency doctor hotline, **Ärztenotdienst**, or go to the nearest hospital (Krankenhaus); the main facility is Vienna General. Most doctors, paramedics and staff speak English.

Ärztenotdienst
☎ 141
GHIC
🌐 ghic.org.uk

Money

Major credit, debit and prepaid currency cards are accepted in most shops and restaurants. Contactless payments are becoming more widely accepted, even on public transport, but it is always wise to carry some cash.

Travellers with Specific Requirements

The majority of the transport system is equipped for use by travellers with reduced mobility and hearing and visual impairments. Many of the buses and trams are street-level vehicles with fold-out ramps and a flashing wheelchair symbol to help visitors identify them, but look for trams with the ULF (Ultra Low Floor) sign. Underground stations are equipped with "guiding stripes" to help visually impaired travellers navigate escalators, exits and lifts. A Braille station map of Vienna's underground system can be purchased from the public transport operator Wiener Linien (p139).

Most major museums are wheelchair accessible and offer audio tours, while many restaurants are also wheelchair accessible and offer disabled parking.

Several companies offer services to visitors with visual and hearing impairments, including **Bizeps**.

Bizeps
🌐 bizeps.or.at

Language

German is Austria's official language, but even those with a good grasp may find the Austrian dialects hard to decipher. English is commonly spoken in Vienna, but learning a few niceties in German goes a long way.

Opening Hours

Museum opening times vary but most are open 10am–5pm, closing on either Monday or Tuesday. Some of the larger attractions stay open late one evening, often until 9pm.

Shops are usually open 9am–6:30pm Monday to Friday and 9am–5pm on Saturday; some shopping centres are open until 8pm or 9pm.

Most banks are open 8am–12:30pm and 1:30–3pm Monday to Friday (to 5:30pm Friday). In the city centre (1st district) banks don't close for lunch.

Restaurants open daily in the city centre, with those in the outer districts closing for one or two days each week.

Situations can change quickly and unexpectedly. Always check before visiting attractions and hospitality venues for up-to-date opening hours and booking requirements.

Personal Security

Vienna is a relatively safe city to visit, but it's always a good idea to take precautions when wandering around the city, particularly at night. Extra care should be taken against pickpockets, particularly on public transport and in busy tourist areas – especially in and around the Prater. If you have anything stolen, report the crime within 24 hours to the nearest police station and take ID with you. Get a copy of the crime report to make an insurance claim. Contact your embassy if you have your passport stolen, or in the event of a serious crime or accident.

As a rule, the Viennese are very accepting of all people, regardless of their race, gender or sexuality. Though LGBTQ+ rights in Austria are less progressive than many European countries, homosexuality has been legal since 1971 and in 2009, Austria recognized the right to legally change your gender. If you do feel unsafe, the welcoming **Türkis Rosa Lila Villa**, an LGBTQ+ community centre and café, acts as a safe space.

Türkis Rosa Lila Villa
W dievilla.at

Smoking, Alcohol and Drugs

Austria used to have one of Europe's highest smoking rates. Following most European nations, smoking was finally banned in Austrian bars and restaurants in November 2019.

It is illegal to drive under the influence of alcohol *(p141)*. There are heavy penalties, jail sentences and fines for drug possession depending on the type of narcotic.

ID

There is no requirement for visitors to carry ID, but in the event of a routine check, you may be asked to show your passport. If you don't have it with you, the police may escort you to wherever your passport is being kept so that you can show it to them.

Responsible Travel

Vienna is one of the world's most sustainable cities and there's plenty you can do to keep it that way. The city has excellent public transport, so take the bus instead of summoning an Uber. Even better, go by bike – there's a bike-sharing scheme for the city's 1,700 km

---

AT A GLANCE

EMERGENCY NUMBERS

GENERAL EMERGENCY	AMBULANCE
112	**144**

FIRE SERVICE	POLICE
122	**133**

TIME ZONE
CET/CEST: Central European Summer Time runs from the last Sunday in March to the last Sunday in October.

TAP WATER
Unless stated otherwise, tap water in Vienna and its surrounds is safe to drink.

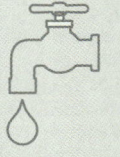

WEBSITES AND APPS

WienMobil
An app that helps you to locate your nearest WienMobil bike rental station.

City of Vienna
This site has a useful interactive city map *(www.wien.gv.at)*.

Qando Wien
The official transport app from Vienna's public transport provider, Wiener Linien.

Susi
This app shows you nearby restaurants, free events, ATMs and pharmacies.

(1,055 miles) of bike paths. When planning a city break, consider visiting in March or November, so as not to contribute to the busy summer season. It's possible to choose climate-neutral accommodation (check your hotel's website). You can even help the wider region's sustainability by taking direct flights to Vienna rather than transiting in Bratislava, which puts strain on neighbouring Slovakia's infrastructure for no economic return.

Check the **Vienna Tourist Board** website before shopping for souvenirs, as it lists places where you can buy sustainable products.

Vienna Tourist Board
W wien.info/en

Mobile Phones and Wi-Fi

Visitors travelling to Austria with EU call plans can use their devices abroad without being affected by data roaming charges; instead, they are charged the same rates for data, SMS and voice calls as they would pay at home. However, visitors who are staying for extensive periods may find buying an inexpensive Austrian prepaid phone or SIM card worthwhile.

Vienna has more than 400 free Wi-Fi hotspots, including train stations and many hotels. The most popular are in Rathausplatz, the Prater, Stephans-platz, the MuseumsQuartier, the Naschmarkt and along the Danube Island. The **City of Vienna** website has an interactive map showing the Wi-Fi hotspots. Cafés and restaurants are usually happy to permit the use of their Wi-Fi on the condition that you make a purchase. Wi-Fi is now almost always free in hotels. You can also get online at the helpful tourist information centre on Albertinaplatz.

City of Vienna
W wien.gv.at

Post

Austria's postal service, established in 1490, is the oldest standardized postal service in Europe. There are two mailing options from Austria to foreign destinations – priority and economy for Europe and the rest of the world. A standard letter (up to 20g) is automatically posted as priority and will reach the UK in a few days and the US in less than a week.

Stamps are sold at all post offices. Red stripes on a yellow post box indicates that they are emptied on Sundays and public holidays. The city's yellow-fronted post offices are open 8am–noon and 2–6pm Monday–Friday (some stay open during lunch). Sub-offices in railway stations are often open 24 hours daily. Find locations and hours on the **Post** website.

Post
W post.at

Taxes and Refunds

VAT is 20 per cent in Austria. Non-EU residents are entitled to a tax refund subject to certain conditions. In order to do this, you must request a tax receipt and export papers (*Ausfuhrbescheinigung*) when you purchase your goods. When leaving the country, present these papers at Customs, along with the receipt and your ID, to receive your refund.

Discount Cards

A useful discount card is Wiener Linien's **Vienna City Card**. A "Red" adult pass costs €17, €25 or €29 for 1, 2 or 3 days and provides free entry into over 60 of Vienna's attractions and museums. The pass also entitles travellers to the unlimited use of hop-on, hop-off buses, a free guidebook and an optional public transport pass. Children's passes cost roughly half of an adult pass.

The **Vienna PASS** (available for 1, 2, 3 or 6 consecutive days) is only good value if you intend to visit numerous sights in a short period of time.

Vienna City Card
W viennacitycard.at
Vienna PASS
W viennapass.de/en

PLACES TO STAY

Vienna has the full range of accommodation options you would expect to find in a European capital, from luxury five-star hotels to backpacker party hostels. Standards are high across the board, and thanks to the compact size of the city, you'll never have to travel far from your hotel to take in the majority of the city's sights. Vienna is fairly pricey all year round, but the highest rates are in the European summer holidays (July and August) and during Advent (the fourth Sunday before Christmas).

PRICE CATEGORIES

For a standard, double room per night (with breakfast if included), taxes and extra charges.

€ under €150
€€ €150–€280
€€€ over €280

Central Vienna

Hotel Astoria
Ⓟ M5 **⌂** Kärntner Strasse 32–34 **ⓦ** astoria-wien.com · €€

This Art Deco gem is back after a full and meticulous revamp, making it one of the top historic hotels in the city. Rooms are a study in period styling, with parquet floors, 1920s-style lighting and original fittings. Breakfast is served in the stylish dining room, and there's an Art Deco bar as well.

Rosewood Vienna
Ⓟ M3 **⌂** Petersplatz 7 **ⓦ** rosewoodhotels.com/en/vienna · €€€

Housed in a beautifully restored 19th-century building, this is arguably Vienna's best hotel, with a prime location – next to Peterskirche church – pristinely designed rooms and a gourmet breakfast. Décor blends historic charm with modern elegance, and there is also fine dining and a wellness spa.

Boutique Hotel Am Stephansplatz
Ⓟ N3 **⌂** Stephansplatz 9 **ⓦ** hotelamstephansplatz.at · €€€

You're right in the thick of the action at this small hotel on Stephansplatz, just steps away from the Stephansdom. Standards are very high, and there's a surprisingly modern design throughout. Try to bag a room overlooking the cathedral.

Hotel Sacher
Ⓟ M5 **⌂** Philharmonikerstrasse 4 **ⓦ** sacher.com · €€€

As the birthplace of the celebrated Sachertorte (p84), this is one of the most famous, and historic, hotels in Vienna. Character-packed rooms combine with service, design and facilities that are all befiting of its lofty status.

Hotel König von Ungarn
Ⓟ P3 **⌂** Schulerstrasse 10 **ⓦ** hvu.at · €€€

Within walking distance of Stephansplatz, the "King of Hungary" hotel maintains very high standards throughout but also has bags of charm, plus the odd quirk, with rooms ranging from wood panelling to retro décor. The hotel makes much of the fact that Mozart once stayed here, composing some of *The Marriage of Figaro* while doing so.

Hotel Bristol
Ⓟ M6 **⌂** Kärntner Ring 1 **ⓦ** marriott.com · €€€

The Bristol is a real luxury treat, a favourite with visiting celebs and the occasional politician. Despite the high price tag, booking a room here can be a tall order, but if you are able to stay here, expect super service and a wide range of facilities.

Hotel Austria Wien
Ⓟ P2 **⌂** Fleischmarkt 20 **ⓦ** hotelaustria-wien.at · €

Located in the centre of the city between the Danube and the Stephansdom, the Austria Wien still enjoys a quiet location, and has reasonably priced, no-frills rooms of a decent standard. Many guests praise the breakfast here which is served in the grand dining room. You can take advantage of a variety of discounts if you book directly through the hotel's own website.

Hotel Nossek
📍 M3 🏠 Graben 17
🌐 boutiquehotel-nosseh.at · €€

This long-standing, olde-worlde guesthouse is located at Vienna's epicentre. For a year (1781–2), it was the home of Mozart, who composed *The Abduction from the Seraglio* here. Today's rooms are comfortingly old fashioned, the welcome is warm and the buffet breakfast is a verified crowd-pleaser. The hotel's setting, on a quiet, pedestrianized street, could not be better.

Hotel Wandl
📍 M3 🏠 Petersplatz 9
🌐 hotel-wandl.com · €€

This family-run inn fills an 18th-century palace that boasts a superb location two blocks from the Stephansdom. If you're in the market for some old-money service, understatedly stylish quarters and a traditional Viennese welcome, look no further. Guests get a very good breakfast, and there's also a dedicated shuttle to and from the airport.

Schottenring and Alsergrund

Hilton Vienna Plaza
📍 B4 🏠 Schottenring 11
🌐 hilton.com · €€

The Hilton Vienna Plaza is set within a spectacular Art Deco-style building, one of the city's most impressive. Rooms are studies in subtle elegance and stylish comfort, while well-trained staff will tend your every need. It's a short walk from here to many of the city's major sights.

H+ Hotel Wien
📍 A3 🏠 Liechtenstein-strasse 87–89 🌐 h-hotels.com · €€

Half hostel, half budget-style four-star hotel with contemporary design elements, this H Hotel has a convenient location in the Alsergrund area near the Franz Josephs train station. There are four standards of room; the lowest priced are frugal but comfortable affairs. The dorm is made up of ten basic, wooden box bunks but is fine for the money, and there's a kitchen for guest use.

Hotel Harmonie
📍 B3 🏠 Harmoniegasse 5
🌐 bestwestern.de · €€

A Best Western property, this small, beautifully designed boutique hotel is a delightful place to stay. The 66 rooms are modern and stylish, with original artwork in each

one. A filling breakfast and traditional Viennese afternoon tea are other plus points. The location, in a quiet side street, ensures a soothing night's sleep.

MuseumsQuartier, Town Hall and Neubau

Hotel MOTTO
📍 F2 🏠 Mariahilfer Strasse 71a 🌐 hotel motto.at · €€€

As the last word in exquisite styling, it's no wonder that the MOTTO is Vienna's top-rated boutique hotel. The generously sized rooms have parquet floors and are stuffed with retro furniture, while the chic décor will offer plenty of inspiration for your own abode. Chez Bernard restaurant on the 7th floor is a cool hangout and has one of the city's best rooftop bars.

Miiro Hotel Maria Theresia
📍 J5 🏠 Kirchberggasse 6
🌐 miirohotels.com/maria-theresia · €€

Part of the hip K+K collection, this crisp, mid-range hotel opened in 2025 on the doorstep of the MuseumsQuartier, putting you in the thick of the arty action. There are 132 shiny rooms, an Italian restaurant and Scandinavian design throughout. And it doesn't come with the hefty price tag you might expect.

Hotel-Pension Museum

9 J5 **A** Museumstrasse 3 **W** hotelmuseum.at · €€

This old-school guest-house has bags of character. As the name suggests, these digs are in the MuseumsQuartier, but they're also well located for many of the city's other sights. Rooms are a touch spartan but have parquet floors and high ceilings, and there's a great breakfast spread.

Opera and Naschmarkt

Hotel zur Wiener Staatsoper

9 N5 **A** Krugerstrasse 11 **W** hotel-staatsoper.at · €€€

No prizes for guessing where this newly renovated, highly exclusive, 100-year-old hotel might be located. With just 12 rooms, an illustrious list of former guests and a winning mix of elegance and impeccable service, this superb place right around the corner from the Vienna State Opera is a classy choice for guests with cash to splash. The suites are some of the finest in central Vienna.

Grand Hotel Wien

9 N6 **A** Kärntner Ring 9 **W** ihg.com · €€€

Sitting proudly on the Ring, this is arguably Vienna's finest luxury hotel, opulent inside and out and within walking distance of all the major central sights. Huge in size and commanding in stature, the aptly named Grand Hotel Wien has five restaurants and bars, a spa, a huge ballroom and several event rooms. Guestrooms are palatial both in size and décor.

JO&JOE Vienna

A Europaplatz 1 **W** joandjoe.com/vienna · €

If you've come to Vienna to let your hair down, then the city's newest (party) hostel is the place to do it. The décor is striking and urban, the atmosphere is youthful and happening, and the location – right next to the Westbahnhof – very convenient. For a hostel, the dorms are amazingly spacious, and the bunks offer higher-than-usual levels of privacy.

Wombat's City Hostel

9 F3 **A** Rechte Wienzeile 35 **W** wombats-hostels.com/vienna · €

This long-established city hostel (part of a mostly Central European hostel chain) occupies an Art Nouveau building right by the Naschmarkt. Private rooms are quite spartan and a little bit overpriced, but the cheapish dorms (some female-only) offer decent value and have bunks with curtains. Breakfast is included and there's a café and a bar on the premises.

O11 Boutique Hotel Vienna

9 L5 **A** Opernring 11 **W** o11-hotel.com · €€€

Situated near the Vienna Opera House on the Ring, this top-draw boutique hotel has soothing Scandi design, understated rooms and well-regimented staff. Some rooms have free-standing baths and come in shades of brown and beige you never knew existed. The Mon Cher restaurant on the premises offers fine French cuisine.

From Karlskirche to the Belvedere

The Hoxton Vienna

9 E6 **A** Rudolf-Sallinger-Platz 1 **W** thehoxton.com/vienna · €€

The first Hoxton Group offering in Vienna, this hip hotel immediately became one of the finest places to stay in the city when it opened in 2024. Clipped and simple 1950s modernism is the theme here with lots of retro-chic and period features. Rooms come in a variety of size, although note that the small rooms are very petit.

Hotel Johann Strauss

9 G4 **A** Favoritenstrasse 12 **W** hoteljohannstrauss.at · €€

Located in the heart of Vienna, this modern hotel is a typically Central European, four-star affair, offering 64 elegant, traditionally styled rooms that come with contemporary facilities. Close to famous attractions like the Belvedere palaces and the Karlskirche, the JS combines a cosy atmosphere and friendly service with convenient access to the city's public transport.

Hotel Kaiserhof

⑨ F4 🏠 Frankenberggasse 10 🅦 wien.hotel-kaiserhof.at · €€€

A solid, no-nonsense hotel, the Kaiserhof upholds the highest standards of traditional accommodation and cuisine – which it has been successfully doing since 1896. From the opulent décor to the grand breakfast room, everything here is done with olde-worlde flair. It's excellently situated for many of the city's sights.

Art Hotel

⑨ H2 🏠 Brandmayergasse 7 🅦 arthotelvienna.at · €

This three-star hotel has an eye-catching façade and splashes of arty colour throughout. There's a mixture of rooms and apartments, some of which come with large, fully equipped kitchens, making this a good choice for those travelling with children. The price-to-quality ratio is very good, although the hotel does sometimes suffer from the odd gremlin.

Greater Vienna

Hotel Schani UNO City

🏠 Wagramer Strasse 16 🅦 schanihotels.com · €€

Opened in 2024, this hotel, the city's third member of the Schani chain, is located in the Vienna International Centre, or UNO City, a hub of United Nations organizations to the northeast of the centre. It offers 200 smart, crisp rooms, each one packed with tech such as smartphone room keys and wireless charging. Some rooms enjoy views over UNO City and the Danube River.

Boutique Hotel Donauwalzer

🏠 Hernalser Gürtel 27 🅦 donauwalzer.at · €

This modern, superbly run hotel has a range of immaculately kept rooms, classical music-themed touches and a much-lauded breakfast. The rooms differ in décor and styling considerably, so ask to view before choosing which one you'd like. It's excellent value for money – and less than 10 minutes from the city centre by public transport.

Austria Classic Hotel Wien

🏠 Praterstrasse 72 🅦 classic-hotelwien.at · €€

This aptly named hotel has classically modern, business-standard rooms and enjoys a convenient location that's away from the city centre but within easy striking distance. Not only is this place good value for money, it also has a list of eco-friendly practices including a electric car charging point and discounts for guests who arrive by train or bike.

JUFA Hotel Wien City

🏠 Mautner-Markhof-Gasse 50 🅦 jufahotels.com · €

Set in the Simmering district, this relatively inexpensive hotel has a beautiful atrium and a management team that really try to take care of their guests. It's an ideal choice for families and business travellers alike, with spacious rooms and a good restaurant, and also conference facilities and easy access to local shops and public transport.

St Christopher's Vienna

🏠 Columbusgasse 16 🅦 st-christophers.co.uk · €

Named after the patron saint of travellers, and located on Columbus Street, this well-kept hostel is a haven for nomads looking for a cheap sleep within touching distance of the city centre. There are big discounts for guests in the hostel's restaurant and a busy calendar of in-house events.

INDEX

PHRASE BOOK

In an Emergency

Where is the telephone?	Wo ist das Telefon?	voh ist duss tel-e-fone?
Help!	Hilfe!	hilf-uh!
Please call a doctor	Bitte rufen Sie einen Arzt	bitt-uh roof'n zee ine-en artst
Please call the police	Bitte rufen Sie die Polizei	bitt-uh roof'n zee dee poli-tsy
Please call the fire brigade	Bitte rufen Sie die Feuerwehr	bitt-uh roof'n zee dee foyer-vayr
Stop!	Halt!	hult!

Communication Essentials

Yes	Ja	yah
No	Nein	nine
Please	Bitte	bitt-uh
Thank you	Danke	dunk-uh
Excuse me	Verzeihung	fair-tsy-hoong
Hello (good day)	Guten Tag	goot-en tahk
Goodbye	Auf Wiedersehn	owf-veed-er-zay-ern
Good evening	Guten Abend	goot'n ahb'nt
Good night	Gute Nacht	goot-uh nukht
Why?	Warum?	var-room?
Where?	Wo?	voh?
When?	Wann?	vunn?
today	Heute	hoyt-uh
tomorrow	Morgen	morg'n
month	Monat	mohn-aht
night	Nacht	nukht
afternoon	Nachmittag	nahkh-mit-tahk
morning	Morgen	morg'n
year	Jahr	yar
there	dort	dort
here	hier	hear
week	Woche	vokh-uh
yesterday	Gestern	gest'n
evening	Abend	ahb'nt

Useful Phrases

How are you?	Wie geht's?	vee gayts?
Fine, thanks	Danke, es geht mir gut	dunk-uh, es gayt meer goot
Where is/are?	Wo ist/sind...?	voh ist/sind?
How far is it to...?	Wie weit ist es...?	vee vite ist ess?
Do you speak English?	Sprechen Sie Englisch?	shpresh'n zee eng-glish?
I don't understand	Ich verstehe nicht	ish fair-shtay-uh nisht
Please speak more slowly	Bitte, sprechen Sie langsamer	bitte shpresh'n zee lang-zammer

Useful Words

large	gross	grohss
small	klein	kline
hot	heiss	hyce
cold	kalt	kult
good	gut	goot
bad	böse/schlecht	burss-uh/shlesht
open	geöffnet	g'urff-nett
closed	geschlossen	g'shloss'n
left	links	links
right	rechts	reshts

Making a Telephone Call

| I would like to make a phone call | Ich möchte telefonieren | ish mer-shtuh tel-e-fon-eer'n |

I'll try again later	Ich versuche noch ein mal später	ish fair-zookh-uh r nokh ine-mull shpay-te
Can I leave a message?	Kann ich eine Nachricht hinterlassen?	kan ish ine-uh nakh-risht hint-er-lahss-en?
telephone card	Telefonkarte	tel-e-fohn-kart-uh
mobile phone	Mobiltelfon	mobeel tel-e-fone
engaged (busy)	besetzt	b'zetst
wrong number	Falsche Verbindung	falsh-uh fair-bin-doong

Sightseeing

entrance ticket	Eintrittskarte	ine-tritz-kart-uh
cemetery	Friedhof	freed-hofe
train station	Bahnhof	barn-hofe
gallery	Galerie	gall-er-ree
information	Auskunft	owss-koonft
church	Kirche	keersh-uh
garden	Garten	gart'n
palace/castle	Palast/Schloss	pallast/shloss
place (square)	Platz	plats
bus stop	Haltestelle	hal-te-shtel-uh
national holiday	Nationalfeiertag	nats-yon-ahl-fire-tahk
theatre	Theater	tay-aht-er
free admission	Eintritt frei	ine-tritt fry

Shopping

Do you have...?	Gibt es...?	geept ess?
How much does it cost?	Was kostet das?	voss kost't duss?
When do you open/close?	Wann öffnen Sie? schliessen Sie?	vunn off'n zee? shlees'n zee?
this	das	duss
expensive	teuer	toy-er
cheap	preiswert	price-vurt
size	Grösse	gruhs-uh
number	Nummer	noom-er
colour	Farbe	farb-uh
brown	braun	brown
black	schwarz	shvarts
red	rot	roht
blue	blau	blau
green	grün	groon
yellow	gelb	gelp

Types of Shop

antiques shop	Antiquariat	antik-var-yat
chemist (pharmacy)	Apotheke/ Drogerie	appo-tay-kuh/ droog-er-ree
bank	Bank	bunk
market	Markt	markt
travel agency	Reisebüro	rye-zer-boo-roe
department store	Warenhaus	vahr'n-hows
hairdresser	Friseur	freezz-er
newspaper kiosk	Zeitungskiosk	tsytoongs-kee-osk
bookshop	Buchhandlung	bookh-hant-loong
bakery	Bäckerei	beck-er-eye
post office	Post	posst
shop/store	Geschäft/Laden	gush-eft/lard'n
shoe shop	Schuhladen	shoo-lard'n
clothes shop	Kleiderladen, Boutique	klyder-lard'n, boo-teek-uh
food shop	Lebensmittelgeschäft	lay-bens-mittel-gush-eft

Staying in a Hotel

Do you have	**Haben Sie noch**	*harb'n zee nokh*
any vacancies?	**Zimmer frei?**	*tsimm-er-fry?*
with twin beds?	**mit zwei Betten?**	*mitt tsvy bett'n?*
with a	**mit einem**	*mitt ine'm*
double bed?	**Doppelbett?**	*dopp'l-bet?*
with a bath?	**mit Bad?**	*mitt bart?*
with a shower?	**mit Dusche?**	*mitt doosh-uh?*
I have a	**Ich habe eine**	*ish harb-uh*
reservation	**Reservierung**	*ine-uh*
		rez-er-veer-oong
key	**Schlüssel**	*shlooss'l*
porter	**Pförtner**	*pfert-ner*

Eating Out

Do you have a	**Haben Sie**	*harb'n zee*
table for …?	**einen Tisch für …?**	*ine-uhn tish foor?*
I would like to	**Ich möchte eine**	*ish mer-shtuh*
reserve a	**Reservierung**	*ine-uh rezer-veer-*
table	**machen**	*oong-makh'n*
Waiter!	**Herr Ober!**	*hair oh-bare!*
The bill (check)	**Die Rechnung**	*dee resh-noong*
breakfast	**Frühstück**	*froo-shtook*
lunch	**Mittagessen**	*mit-tag-ess'n*
dinner	**Abendessen**	*arb'nt-ess'n*
bottle	**Flasche**	*flush-uh*
dish of the day	**Tagesgericht**	*tahgs-gur-isht*
main dish	**Hauptgericht**	*howpt-gur-isht*
dessert	**Nachtisch**	*nahkh-tish*
cup	**Tasse**	*tass-uh*
wine list	**Weinkarte**	*vine-kart-uh*
glass	**Glas**	*glars*
spoon	**Löffel**	*lerff'l*
tip	**Trinkgeld**	*trink-gelt*
knife	**Messer**	*mess-er*
starter	**Vorspeise**	*for-shpize-uh*
(appetizer)		
plate	**Teller**	*tell-er*
fork	**Gabel**	*gahb'l*

Menu Decoder

Beefsteack	*beef-stayk*	steak
Bier	*beer*	beer
Branntwein	*brant-vine*	spirits
Bratkartoffeln	*brat-kar-toff'ln*	fried potatoes
Bratwurst	*brat-voorst*	fried sausage
Brötchen	*bret-tchen*	bread roll
Brot	*brot*	bread
Brühe	*bruh-uh*	broth
Butter	*boot-ter*	butter
Champignon	*shum-pin-yong*	mushroom
Ei	*eye*	egg
Eis	*ice*	ice/ice cream
Ente	*ent-uh*	duck
Fisch	*fish*	fish
Forelle	*for-ell-uh*	trout
Frikadelle	*Frika-dayl-uh*	hamburger
Gans	*ganns*	goose
Garnele	*gar-nayl-uh*	prawn/shrimp
gebraten	*g'braat'n*	fried
gegrillt	*g'grilt*	grilled
gekocht	*g'kokht*	boiled
geräuchert	*g'rowk-ert*	smoked
Gemüse	*g'mooz-uh*	vegetables
Hähnchen	*haynsh'n*	chicken
Kaffee	*kaf-fay*	coffee
Kalbfleisch	*kalp-flysh*	veal
Karpfen	*karpf'n*	carp
Käse	*kayz-uh*	cheese
Knoblauch	*k'nob-lowkh*	garlic
Knödel	*k'nerd'l*	noodle
Kohl	*koal*	cabbage
Kuchen	*kookh'n*	cake
Milch	*milsh*	milk
Mineralwasser	*minn-er-arl-*	mineral water
	vuss-er	
Öl	*erl*	oil
Pfeffer	*pfeff-er*	pepper
Rindfleisch	*rint-flysh*	beef
Saft	*zuft*	juice
Salat	*zal-aat*	salad
Salz	*zults*	salt
Salzkartoffeln	*zults-kar-toff'l*	boiled potatoes
Sekt	*zekt*	sparkling wine
scharf	*sharf*	spicy
Schnitzel	*shnitz'l*	veal/pork cutlet
Schweinefleisch	*shvine-flysh*	pork
Spargel	*shparg'l*	asparagus
Spinat	*shpin-art*	spinach
Tee	*tay*	tea
Wein	*vine*	wine
Wiener	*veen-er*	frankfurter
Würstchen	*voorst-sh'n*	
Zucker	*tsook-er*	sugar
Zwiebel	*tsveeb'l*	onion

Numbers

0	**null**	*nool*
1	**eins**	*eye'ns*
2	**zwei**	*tsvy*
3	**drei**	*dry*
4	**vier**	*feer*
5	**fünf**	*foonf*
6	**sechs**	*zex*
7	**sieben**	*zeeb'n*
8	**acht**	*uhkht*
9	**neun**	*noyn*
10	**zehn**	*tsayn*
11	**elf**	*elf*
12	**zwölf**	*tserlf*
13	**dreizehn**	*dry-tsayn*
14	**vierzehn**	*feer-tsayn*
15	**fünfzehn**	*foonf-tsayn*
16	**sechzehn**	*zex-tsayn*
17	**siebzehn**	*zeep-tsayn*
18	**achtzehn**	*uhkht-tsayn*
19	**neunzehn**	*noyn-tsayn*
20	**zwanzig**	*tsvunn-tsig*
21	**einundzwanzig**	*ine-oont-tsvunn-tsig*
30	**dreissig**	*dry-sig*
40	**vierzig**	*feer-sig*
50	**fünfzig**	*foonf-tsig*
60	**sechzig**	*zex-tsig*
70	**siebzig**	*zeep-tsig*
80	**achtzig**	*uhkht-tsig*
90	**neunzig**	*noyn-tsig*
100	**hundert**	*hoond't*
1,000	**tausend**	*towz'nt*
1,000,000	**eine Million**	*ine-uh mill-yon*

Time

one minute	**eine Minute**	*ine-uh*
		min-oot-uh
one hour	**eine Stunde**	*ine-uh*
		shtoond-uh
Monday	**Montag**	*mohn-targ*
Tuesday	**Dienstag**	*deens-targ*
Wednesday	**Mittwoch**	*mitt-vokh*
Thursday	**Donnerstag**	*donn-ers-targ*
Friday	**Freitag**	*fry-targ*
Saturday	**Samstag**	*zums-targ*
Sunday	**Sonntag**	*zon-targ*

ACKNOWLEDGMENTS

This edition updated by

Contributor Marc di Duca

Senior Editor Keith Drew

Senior Designer Stuti Tiwari

Project Art Editor Divyanshi Shreyaskar

Editors Tavleen Kaur, Ilina Choudhary

Proofreader Ben Ffrancon Dowds

Indexer Helen Peters

Picture Researcher Deputy Manager Virien Chopra

Senior Picture Researcher Nishwan Rasool

Assistant Picture Research Administrator Manpreet Kaur

Publishing Assistant Simona Velikova

Jacket Designers Laura O'Brien, Divyanshi Shreyaskar

Jacket Picture Researcher Laura O'Brien

Project Cartographer Ashif

Senior Cartographing Editor James Macdonald

Cartography Manager Suresh Kumar

Pre-production Coordinator Tanveer Zaidi

Pre-production Designer Rohit Rojal

Pre-production Image Editor Mohd Rizwan

Pre-production Manager Balwant Singh

Image Retouching Production Manager Pankaj Sharma

Senior Production Controller Kariss Ainsworth

Deputy Managing Editor Dharini Ganesh

Managing Editor Beverly Smart

Managing Art Editor Gemma Doyle

Senior Managing Art Editor Priyanka Thakur

Editorial Director Hollie Teague

Art Director Maxine Pedliham

Publishing Director Georgina Dee

DK would like to thank the following for their contribution to the previous editions: Kathryn Glendenning, Michael Leidig, Melanie Nicholson-Hartzell, Clive Streeter, Peter Wilson, Sarah Woods, Irene Zoech

The publisher would like to thank the following for their kind permission to reproduce their photographs:

Key: a-above; b-below/bottom; c-center; f-far; l-left; r-right; t-top

123RF.com: tasfoto 83t.

Adobe Stock: David Brown 15clb; visualpower 1.

Alamy Stock Photo: APA-PictureDesk 10tl, 12crb, 73t, 119, 125t; ART Collection 8–9b; bozac 16tc; Michael Brooks 16c; Chronicle 9tr; Carol Di Rienzo Cornwell 77cr; Ian Dagnall 76b, 113; Directphoto Collection 100; Peter Adams / DanitaDelimont.com 22; Dpa Picture Alliance 11b; Markus Scholz / dpa 102, EDR archives 10tr; eFesenko 81t, 81b; Fine Art Images / Heritage Images 66t; Luisa Fumi 9cr; Manfred Gottschalk 48; GRANGER Historical Picture Archive 39b; Hackenberg-Photo-Cologne 103b; Borgese Maurizio / Hemis.fr 91t; Gardel Bertrand / Hemis. fr 62–63, 87b; Image Professionals GmbH / LOOK-foto 12br, 126; Image Professionals GmbH / Ingolf Pompe 109; imageBROKER.com / Egon Bömsch 40b; imageBROKER / Rolf Fischer 26–27t; imageBROKER / Raimund Franken 53; imageBROKER / Petr Svarc 21c; Imagedoc 15t, 28; IMAGO / Harald A. Jahn 15bc; Jon Arnold Images Ltd / Neil Farrin 96b; John Kellerman 33b, 111b; Graham Salter / Lebrecht Music & Arts 23cb; Marco Maraviglia 73b; Stefano Politi Markovina 122; mauritius images GmbH / Volker Preusser 13cl (8), 83b; McPhoto / Bilderbox 24; Tim Moore 17; MWE 111t; Penta Springs Limited / Artokoloro 84t; Franz Perc 21b; Petr.F 14; The Picture Art Collection 31t; The Print Collector / Heritage Images 8t; Matthias Riedinger 75t; robertharding / Jean Brooks 65t; Peter Schickert 66b; Alfred Strobel / Süddeutsche Zeitung Photo 10cl; Patrik Uhlir / CTK 90–91b; VM / BT 127; volkerpreusser 12cra, 13tl, 64, 74, 82, 134; World History Archive 9br.

AWL Images: Jon Arnold 23br, 46cl, 137; Hemis 19, 70b; Stefano Politi Markovina 6–7, 37; Jan Miracky 125b; Ken Scicluna 60, Jane Sweeney 47t.

Belvedere, Vienna: 39t.

Bridgeman Images: 31b.

Café Do-An: 123.

Das Mbel: 114t.

Der Dritte Mann Tour: Felicitas Matern 69.

Dreamstime.com: 22tomtom 78t; Igor Abramovych 49b; Anton Aleksenko 15crb;

Andrei Antipov 87t; Eakkapan Asavapanumas 79b; Bojang 96t; Arkadi Bojarinov 11t, 12cr; Boris Breytman 70t; Cristi Croitoru 65b; Davidzean 98; Demerzel21 36bl; Dudlajzov 57t; Mindaugas Dulinskas 49t; Darius Dzinnik 78b; Giuseppemasci 26b; H368kf742 132t; Kabvisio 79t; Mirko Kuzmanovic 44; Fabio Lotti 21t; Meinzahn 68, 108, 120–121b; Mistervlad 13cl, 20c, 42, 56, 105t; Mitzobs 58–59t; Koba Samurkasov 105b; Belen Sanma 52; Jozef Sedmak 116–117, 117cr; Svetlana195 59; Timelynx 45t; Transurfer343 35b; Vvoevale 13clb, 23bl.

Fabios: 103t.

Getty Images: AFP / Dieter Nagl / Stringer 88; adoc-photos / Corbis 29; DEA / A. Dagli Orti / De Agostini 67; Godong / Universal Images Group 80t; Hulton Archive / brandstaetter images / Imagno 25c; The Image Bank Unreleased / Jorg Greuel 50–51t; The Image Bank Unreleased / Izzet Keribar 85b; Imagno / Hulton Archive / brandstaetter images 36cb; Imagno / Hulton Fine Art Collection / brandstaetter images 38; Moment / Alexander Spatari 5, 10bl; RooM / SilvanBachmann 40–41t; Stone / Walter Bibikow 55; Stone / Pascal Deloche 131; Stone / Jorg Greuel 45b; ullstein bild Dtl. 25b.

Getty Images / iStock: AlexandreFagundes 41b; BrendanHunter 36br; E+ / Chunyip Wong 93; Orietta Gaspari 20b; MichaelUtech 86; Sjo 16cra.

Haus der Musik: Rudi Froese 61.

ImPulsTanz: Karolina Miernik 90t.

© KHM-Museumsverband: 32, 33t, 34, 35t.

Leopold Museum, Vienna: WienTourismus / Peter Rigaud 43t.

Marionettentheater Schloss Schönbrunn: Roman Gerhardt 76t.

Meinl am Graben: Herbert Lehmann 99.

Meixner's Gastwirtschaft: 135.

MuseumsQuartier E+B GesmbH: 112.

Salm Bräu: Mario Kranabetter 128.

Copyright Schloss Schönbrunn Kultur- und Betriebsges.m.b.H: 51b.

Shutterstock.com: Andrei Antipov 80b; Ungvari Attila 85t; Vitold Drutel 106–107; ecstk22 95; Frank Fell Media 117tr; LON 13bl; Mitzo 57b; novama 132–133b; Photoillustrator 72; Elena Pominova 84b; Alessandro Tortora 13cla; trabantos 89.

Sky Bar: 101.

Spanish Riding School: ASAblanca.com / Rene é van Bakel 30t; Mathias Lauringer 30b.

Tunnel: 115.

Vienna Secession: Oliver Ottenschlaeger 46–47b.

Wieden Bräu: 129.

Wien Museum: Lisa Rastl 75b.

Zoom Kindermuseum: J. J. Kucek 43cr.

Cover Images

Front and Spine: **Getty Images:** Moment / Pintai Suchachaisri.

Back: **Alamy Stock Photo:** Peter Adams / DanitaDelimont.com tl; **Dreamstime.com:** Mistervlad cl; **Shutterstock.com:** ecstk22 tr.

Sheet Map Cover Images
Getty Images: Moment / Pintai Suchachaisri.

A NOTE FROM DK

The rate at which the world is changing is constantly keeping the DK Travel team on our toes. While we've worked hard to ensure that this edition of Vienna is accurate and up-to-date, we know that opening hours alter, standards shift, prices fluctuate, places close and new ones pop up in their stead. So, if you notice we've got something wrong or left something out, we want to hear about it. Please get in touch at travelguides@dk.com.

Within each Top 10 list in this book, no hierarchy of quality or popularity is implied. All 10 are, in the editor's opinion, of roughly equal merit.

First edition 2003

Published in Great Britain by Dorling
Kindersley Limited, DK, 20 Vauxhall Bridge Road,
London SW1V 2SA

The authorised representative in the EEA is
Dorling Kindersley Verlag GmbH. Arnulfstr.
124, 80636 Munich, Germany

Published in the United States by DK Publishing,
1745 Broadway, 20th Floor, New York, NY 10019, USA

Copyright © 2003, 2025 Dorling Kindersley Limited
A Penguin Random House Company

25 26 27 28 10 9 8 7 6 5 4 3 2 1

All rights reserved.

No part of this publication may be reproduced, stored in
or introduced into a retrieval system, or transmitted, in any
form, or by any means (electronic, mechanical, photocopying,
recording, or otherwise), without the prior written permission
of the copyright owner.

DK values and supports copyright. Thank you for respecting
intellectual property laws by not reproducing, scanning or
distributing any part of this publication by any means without
permission. By purchasing an authorised edition, you are
supporting writers and artists and enabling DK to continue
to publish books that inform and inspire readers.
No part of this publication may be used or reproduced in any
manner for the purpose of training artificial intelligence
technologies or systems. In accordance with Article 4(3)
of the DSM Directive 2019/790, DK expressly reserves this
work from the text and data mining exception.

The publishers cannot accept responsibility for any consequences
arising from the use of this book, nor for any material on third
party websites, and cannot guarantee that any website address in
this book will be a suitable source of travel information.

A CIP catalog record for this book
is available from the British Library.

A catalog record for this book is available
from the Library of Congress.

ISSN: 1479 344X
ISBN: 978 0 2417 3853 5

Printed and bound in China

www.dk.com

MIX
Paper | Supporting
responsible forestry
FSC™ C018179

This book was made with Forest
Stewardship Council™ certified
paper – one small step in DK's
commitment to a sustainable future.
Learn more at **www.dk.com/uk/
information/sustainability**